EXPERIENCING GOD IN A SECULAR WORLD

Ian Stuchbery

Hamilton Books
A member of
The Rowman & Littlefield Publishing Group
Lanham · Boulder · New York · Toronto · Plymouth, UK

Copyright © 2011 by
Hamilton Books
4501 Forbes Boulevard
Suite 200
Lanham, Maryland 20706
Hamilton Books Acquisitions Department (301) 459-3366

Estover Road
Plymouth PL6 7PY
United Kingdom

All rights reserved

British Library Cataloging in Publication Information Available

Library of Congress Control Number: 2011923604
ISBN: 978-0-7618-5498-2 (paperback : alk. paper)
eISBN: 978-0-7618-5499-9

Contents

Preface	v
Acknowledgement	vii
Chapter 1 The Challenge of the Secular	1
Chapter 2 The Challenge: "There Is No God"	11
Chapter 3 Is the Bible True?	19
Chapter 4 The Jesus of History	27
Chapter 5 Experience: The Golden Thread	41
Chapter 6 Personal Transformation—The Problem: Human Sin	51
Chapter 7 The Kingdom of God: The Vision of a Transformed World	61
Chapter 8 Something More	73
Some Biblical Words	79
The Author	81

Preface

I have been led to write this book by the growing concern of many, about the growth of *secularism* in today's society, particularly in the *Western culture* in which many of us are living. It is aimed specifically at the many men and women who are questioning the reality and relevance of God both within and without the Christian Churches. I hope that it will be especially helpful and encouraging not only to churchgoers who continue to take part in Sunday worship, maybe with many questions in their minds, but also the many others whose personal faith has waned and even some who have long given up any kind of belief in God.

My aim is to get to the very heart of the faith, which I have called the "Golden Thread" of experience; an experience of the divine who lives at the root of all true religion, including the Christian faith. Because this experience is so basic and has figured so consistently in my own personal life and in my ministry as a priest, I have included a number of such experiences. These have been encountered, in both my life and in those of many others. In what follows, I am not only offering my own rational arguments for the reality of the God, as revealed in the person of a man called Jesus, but also the living reality of that God experienced in the lives of men and women today, including myself and my family.

Ian Stuchbery,
Nova Scotia, Canada.
March 2010

Acknowledgement

I would like to acknowledge the welcome contributions of my artistic friend Jennifer Brown for her imagination in drawing the delightful illustrations in chapter six and also Deborah Seary and Cindy MacDonald for all their help in preparing the book for its final printing. My sincere thanks to you all.

Chapter 1
The Challenge of the Secular

As a child, going to church was very much a part of my life. My uncle was a parish priest and after the bombing of my parents' home in London during the Second World War my parents and I went to live with him and his wife in their vicarage, out in the countryside. The parish church was just across the common and it became part of my young life, even when we moved to our own house just a few miles away. I enjoyed singing in the choir and learned how to *serve* at the altar. I was lead to experience the reality of the *Something More* through and beyond the symbols of the odour of incense, the trappings and colours of the worship and the music of the choir. As I grew up, I went to a local school where there was daily worship to begin each day. As I grew older I left and went to a boarding school where *chapel* was part of the course. I enjoyed the singing in its well-trained choir and learned to like the grand religious music of past and present. I continue to treasure those days but, as I have grown older, I have come to realize that much of what I had experienced was in fact a part of the culture of the day, although I still remember it with affection. But it is a culture which is almost nonexistent in today's society. This culture of my youth has radically changed over the years. In today's world, God has little part or relevance in day to day living.

Going to church on Sundays is now a thing of the past for a growing number of people in today's society. Church bells may still ring but those heeding the call are radically fewer in number. In many churches the majority of people filling the pews are older. Religion is no longer taught at school and daily prayer is a thing of the past. Many church buildings have been closed and Sunday, for many, has become a day for shopping and sports events. It is a world of the *secular*, a world in which God has little relevance and who for the majority is no more than a figment of the imagination.

As a priest, I have been faced with the basic question, "Is God Dead?"; "Is there, in fact, a *Something More* to whom we can relate and whom we can experience?" In response to this, I have come to realize that so much of our traditional *religion* is of human making. The ways we worship on Sundays are of our own creation (i.e. we wrote the hymns and orders of service and translated the many different interpretations of the Bible.) How we describe God's *being* is expressed through our human minds. The music we sing is written by men and women, the trappings we use are often much like a Shakespearian play, the words we use are written in human language from many different times according to many different cultures. All are the creation of men and women who have reflected the culture and theology of their own particular time. The Anglican Prayer Book with which I grew up was written by men five hundred years ago. The glorious clothes worn by the clergy go back to a culture that is even more ancient. Many of our hymns go back many centuries and express the cultures and theology of long ago. Incense was used originally partly to get rid of the smells of ancient times! The reality is that all of these traditions were manmade and reflect the cultures of their own times. All too often, they have come to be worshipped in their own right, even though so many are irrelevant in the culture of today's secular society. The inevitable question that arises is this —where is God in today's society? Take away the trappings and what is left? Is there in fact a *Something More*? If there is, then how is it to be not only understood, but actually experienced? How can we be connected to this *Something More*? Can our lives be changed and renewed as we come to experience and know this reality which we call God? What is the relevance of this *God* in the wider world in which we all live? These are questions which need to be asked both by many who are members of the church and partake in worship every Sunday and by many others who have either drifted away from it or have never been through a church door at all.

Many people today simply do not see any kind of reality other than that which they experience in their daily lives on this physical planet. That's it and there is simply nothing more. As a result they go about their daily lives oblivious to the possibility of any other kind of reality. The effects of scientific thinking have indeed left a significant mark on how people think of such things today. Just what has led to this way of thinking, which is anything but new, although its impact is increasing day by day? It poses a challenge which is moving in on us like an incoming tide, threatening to wash away many of our traditional ways of thinking about the reality of the world which we experience day by day. It is the challenge of the *secular* which is not new but goes back for over two millennia, even before the time of Christ. Its beginnings mark the time when people first began to focus their attention, not on the gods that ordered their world, but upon the actual physical world itself, a world we now call the *secular*, a world which can be measured and fashioned, a world of wealth and poverty, of machines and *things*. It is the world quite apart from any god. It is the natural world which we inhabit and investigate, the physical world which the scientist Bernard Lovell once described as that "to which Quantum theory and relativity apply, it is the known world, the world of science and technology." It does not of itself reject the reality of *Something More* but, like an incoming tide, it is causing many in today's society to ask the question "Is the secular world and way of looking at things all that there is?" It is this increasing impact of the secular which undergirds the changes that are taking place today.

Chapter 1

Just What Is Going On?

In the village of my youth, referred to earlier, my uncle was the typical English parson and the church (together with the nearby pub!) was an intrinsic part of the local village life. Everyone recognized my uncle as he strode across the common to church, his cassock flying in the breeze and greeted him with "Morning Vicar" as they passed by. The church played a key role in the social life of the village. Society shared a common heritage and God's benevolent reality was assured. Although this memory is no doubt somewhat rosier than it was in fact, it expressed a reality which has now totally ceased to exist in the popular culture of the Western world as it is today. In fact, it had ceased long ago in the more industrialized parts of England and other countries, even in those days. In a significant book written by the English Bishop Wickham in the 1960s, he revealed the result of studies of his own industrial city in the North of the country, indicating from records going back to the middle of the eighteenth century that the vast proportion of its inhabitants had never been attached to any kind of church. This almost catastrophic collapse was a result of the industrial revolution which brutally destroyed the rural and traditional culture, within which the Christian faith was deeply embedded, and substituted for it a new culture within which God had no place. Although this was not true for the greater part of England (and certainly this rapid breakdown did not happen to any such degree in Canada and the United States), it is clear that something had caused this breakup of the beliefs and lifestyles of the past. What is relevant right now, at the beginning of the 21st century, is that a massive change occurred, a shift that has affected the whole Western culture in which we live today. One of the indicators of this change is the powerful defensive reaction, called *fundamentalism*, which is especially prevalent in some parts of the Church. Something has clearly taken place which is threatening to shift *God* right off the horizon. What we are talking about is the growing influence of secularism which is rapidly infecting our society and its attitudes toward life.

A Confusion of Words

At this stage, it is important that we should take a pause to be quite clear as to exactly what we are talking about when we use this much maligned word *secular*. To some of us it is a negative word used as something to be blamed for everything wrong that seems to threaten our everyday world. Certainly, it is a dirty word to many, but to many others, including many practicing Christians; it can also be a word of challenge and hope. The reason for this confusion is that there are actually three words, all of which come from the same root, and we need to understand their separate meanings. The words are *secular, secularization* and *secularism*. The first of these, *secular*, is a simple word meaning *worldly*, the things pertaining to this world rather than any other kind of reality.

It is the world of science and everyday life. *Secularization* refers to a process, a process in which the secular or *worldly* things begin to take over and dominate the way we live our lives. In the traditional and pre-scientific way of looking at things, humankind attributed almost everything to the one god or, before that, to the unseen powers that dominated their lives. For instance, the great wave, that was reported to have destroyed the Egyptian army at the crossing of the Red Sea and so left the way free for the escaping Jews, was attributed to the intervention of God. (Exodus 14.15 ff) Equally, it was deemed to be the wrath of God that led to the swallowing up of the inhabitants of Gomorrah (Exodus 14.15) rather than an example of volcanic activity. These are examples of how the results of scientific studies of geology have possibly explained the actions of an angry god! Today we do not look to a divine power to destroy our enemies, to cope with our road accidents or wipe out the plague of malaria. We use the more *worldly* methods such as calling an ambulance, injecting an appropriate drug or even dropping a bomb! This is not to say that prayer is not real but it would not count as a secular way of dealing with our problems. I want to emphasize that secularization has diminished the role of God, so that God has become increasingly peripheral in many of our lives and in the world in which we live.

The third word is *secularism*. Actually, it is simply another word for *atheism* which, of course, means *no god*. To believe in secularism is simply to believe that the only reality is the physical world, the world we live in and the huge universe in which it is set. Secularism believes that there is only one way of understanding and describing the *world*, from the smallest particle to vastness of the universe. Secularism assumes that this is the way of science and that there is no room in it for God or any other reality. The concept of there being some kind of *God* is deemed to be no more than an object of human imagination by many in today's society. The American theologian Harvey Cox comments succinctly and powerfully when he writes, "Secularism is the name for an ideology, a new closed world view which functions very much like a religion. Like any other 'ism,' it must therefore be watched carefully to prevent its becoming the ideology of the new establishment."[1]

The Roots and Impact of the Secular

The growing focus on the physical world began over two thousand years ago in Greece when a huge step forward was made in the way in which we humans think about ourselves and the world we live in. It was triggered by the teachings of a philosopher called Aristotle, who shifted the focus of thinking from the hidden world of the unseen gods to the purely *physical* world around us. This was the world to which he looked for both understanding and knowledge. It was the world of things and people, the world of the material or physical world. He and his followers began to explore and define this world, a world of physics and mathematics, a world that could be measured and weighed rather than a world controlled by unseen gods. At the time, his influence was largely limited to the school of philosophy in Athens, but his way of thinking was later to provide the first seeds of the physical study of the world, a world we now call the secular. However, though important, the influence of his teaching remained limited, continuing only in and around the ancient Egyptian city of Alexandria. There it had an important influence on the early Christians, especially in what we now call the Orthodox churches of the Middle East. However, in Europe, it went effectively underground as a result of the spread of Islam in the seventh century and was almost forgotten. For many hundreds of years Aristotle's original thinking was all but lost within the European Christian Church. During what used to be called the *Dark Ages* (i.e. approximately 600 to 1200), the thinking of the Christian Church in Europe was focused almost entirely on the nonphysical world, the world overseen by a god who was *up there*, a world faced with the realities of heaven and hell and all that went with them. It was a mindset in which the physical world was not a priority. God reigned supreme. We see it expressed in the mediaeval world of Chaucer in the 15th century, and of the wonderful English "Mystery Plays" which certainly combined often bawdy language and the everyday worldly liveliness with a backcloth of the overriding reality of the divine. In the same way, the epic of Dante's *Inferno* left no doubt about the overwhelming reality and role of God in this very human world. It was an age of plague and pestilence in which attention was focused on the wrath of God and the dominance of unseen powers. It was also an age when both peasants and kings sought to placate a fearsome deity with everything from penances and pilgrimages to pogroms and crusades. The physical world was seen often crudely as *God's world* and religion was very much a part, if not the centre, of people's lives.

Then, in the 16th century, a wave of new thinking hit Europe which came to be called the Renaissance—a word which simply means *rebirth*, a rebirth of the ancient insights going back to Aristotle and the schools he founded. The effect of this renewal was not greeted with great pleasure by the church of the time and, at first, the new thinking about the *secular* world met stiff opposition. It posed a direct threat to the beliefs and teachings of the mediaeval church. It was conceived as an attack on the idea that the *world* and all things *worldly* were both dangerous and evil. The new thinking focused, not on the divine or the powerful images of heaven and hell but rather upon the physical world, the world in which people lived, a world which could be measured in terms of time and space, a world of science whose reality could be verified and measured by such methods as mathematics and physical observation—in a word, the world of the *secular*. It is not surprising that the new thinking met with fierce and continuing opposition from the Church.

In 1600 the Italian philosopher Giordano Bruno was burned at the stake by the Catholic Church for his *heretical* new scientific teaching. Thirty years later Galileo was condemned by the papal inquisition for propagating the *heresy* that the earth is not the centre of the universe. He was forced to retract his beliefs before the Papal inquisition and was sentenced to permanent house arrest. Gradually the church began to accept this new understanding of the world, the world of the secular. It was expressed in a variety of forms. It is to be seen not only in the growing development of what we now call *science* but in the explosion of artistic design, from the sculptures of Michelangelo to the murals of fra Angelico and the buildings of Brunichello, from the drawings and engineering creations of Leonardo da Vinci to the impressive number of brilliant frescoes decorating the churches and monasteries of Europe. The period of the Renaissance (or *rebirth*) was when the creative minds of the time were exhibiting a breakout from the traditional ways of looking at the world and coming to see it with new insight; the world of the *secular*.

Certainly they did not give up their awareness of the *Something More* but a new wave of thinking had begun, expressed not only by the new awareness of the world as it was in daily life, a new way of looking at the world which has continued to grow and challenge the religious ways of thinking, a wave which I call the process of *Secularization*. It was a new way of looking at the physical world, not just as a pointer to heavenly things but as a reality in itself. In the world of art, the mystery of perspective was solved, making it possible to make things appear to come close or to disappear into the distance. Peoples' faces began to be painted as they really were rather than images of otherworldly figures. I have a vivid memory of standing in front of a beautiful fresco in the quadrangle of a small Franciscan monastery in Tuscany depicting the Virgin Mary ascending into heaven. All the peoples' faces were in an attitude of total awe, staring with rapt attention at the Holy Virgin—but with one exception. It was the face of a simple friar with his face turned back to face all of us who were watching. It was a self portrait of the artist and he had a wonderfully worldly twinkle in his eyes. It was a wicked smile, clearly taking a big dig at all the religiosity of his superiors! He was clearly revealing a new focus, the daily world of the secular.

Since the breakthrough in the 17th century, the impact of secularization has been steadily increasing, at first slowly but in recent years with increasing rapidity. Throughout the Western world we have welcomed the amazing discoveries and applications of science (although sometimes this has led to some legitimate concern and debate). Our quality of life has been vastly enhanced, not the least by the impact of the marvels of modern medicine. We have come to have a deeper experience of living in this amazing world, a physical world in which we, as *believers* can sense God's presence. All this is good. As St. Francis saw back in the Middle Ages, this *secular* world we are living in is God's most amazing creation, a physical world in which we can "see God's hand." All this is good, yet there is a dark side, as we are increasingly coming to realize. *Secularization*, when it threatens to deny the Something More, is not a good thing.

The Growing Threat of the Secular

Step by step this wave grew from the 17th century onwards, until it arrived at a point when the reality of the divine began to be not only challenged but rejected altogether. As the French scientist Laplace very pithily declaimed about the existence of God, "I have no need of that hypothesis." From that point the wave has continued to grow with force and increasing speed into our own day, a reality which I have no need to elaborate. This denial of God was to have its full impact over the last century. Just after the First World War, Karl Marx was to write his *Das Kapital*, leading to the rapid rise of atheistic communism, which led to the forcible banishment of all religion, not only in the new USSR, but of the whole of Eastern Europe that was overrun by the Russians at the end of World War II.

The church buildings were all destroyed, Christian leaders were executed, millions of the faithful perished. God was forcibly declared "no more!" Thankfully, such a violent and enforced atheism ended, but the wave of secularism (i.e. anti-religion) has continued. More and more citizens of the Western world are becoming victims of this increasing wave of secularism. Signs of this impact are all around us as we continue to see. In our own country, Canada, as we have seen, religion is rarely taught or even mentioned in its schools, Sundays are no longer days of rest, religious insignia is becoming suspect . . . the list could go on. The Christian faith in God is certainly under increasing attack in today's Western society.

The Christian Response

To sum up, just what should be the Christian response? I suggest that it should be twofold. First of all we need to accept and appreciate the reality of our own secular and physical world, with all the insights of modern science which have transformed our understanding of the physical world over the past few hundreds of years. Despite the negative effects of technology when misused, the secular has brought vast improvements to the health and lifestyles of much of our human society.

Back in the 1960's, the English scholar (and one of my teachers) John Robinson published a book called *Honest to God* [2] which caused a considerable stir in the country. He himself was a committed Christian and, in fact one of my teachers at Cambridge, but the point he was making was that the idea of the *Something More* was becoming increasingly ignored in the culture of modern society. He saw the spreading of aggressive disbelief on the horizon. This is indeed the challenge that all of us who are people of faith are being forced to confront. One unfortunate response today is to demonize the secular, which is one of the mistakes of fundamentalism which tends to interpret the secular as somehow essentially evil, whereas in fact it is neither good nor bad. This is a point that was also very powerfully shown in the works of Harvey Cox, whose book *The Secular City* provides a sweeping study of the development of the secular in today's Western world. Although the book is decidedly *60's*, it powerfully sheds light on the ways our culture has continued to develop, often quite dramatically, over the intervening years. What made the work so helpful to many like me was that, instead of describing the growing secularization as inherently negative or destructive, he helped us get a better understanding of how secularization does not necessarily imply something bad—which it certainly is not. One can write an extremely long list of the destruction it has caused, from the horror of nuclear weapons to the poisoning of the atmosphere by carbon emissions. However there is also much that has lead to a better quality of life in our society and vast advances have been achieved in the *physical* sciences. Cox's book makes it clear that the discoveries and applications of today's secular world can become sources of enhanced qualities of life and, if we use them creatively, as a means to learn how to live in a way that will allow the continuance of our human species.

Up to this point, I have deliberately been speaking largely of the so-called *Western world* and ignoring the rapid growth of Christianity in many other parts of the world. This has led to an increasing focus on what some are calling the growing *Church*, especially in Africa, South America and many parts of Asia. In these parts of the world, church numbers continue to expand and God is a reality in people's daily lives. All of this raises many questions of what *Christianity* might be like as we enter into the coming 21st century. What is our vision of the future of our churches as we look ahead, especially in the so-called Western world?

In the Western world we are asking how we are to deal with the diminishing numbers of people in many of our churches. How are we to envision *God* in a world of science and technology and just what is the relevance of worship and prayer in our own daily lives?

All of this is challenged powerfully by such extreme voices as that of Richard Dawkins in his book *The God Delusion* on which I expand in chapter two and, to a lesser degree in the position expressed by Gretta Vosper[3] and others of an extreme liberal orientation in the church. It is these views which have led me to the writing of this book. I also make the point that, not only is there a very large number of scientists today who believe in the reality of God, but also that scientific evidence in the field of contemporary research, in both molecular and quantum levels, clearly point to intelligent design in creation. Certainly I also try to show the *secular* as a practical and realistic way of looking at our physical world and to suggest that it is a reality to be fully embraced as we try to live in it, despite all the challenges it provides. It is the world we live in day by day and from which we look forward in hope. As the French scientist Teilard de Chardin (1881-1955) once put it when he wrote: "The Faith of Mankind as well as religion depends on the emergence of a new faith in the future of the secular world."[4] However I am emphasizing that beyond the secular there is *another reality* which is the *Something More* which we call God. As William Shakespeare might have observed in Macbeth: "There are more things in heaven and earth, Dr. Dawkins, than are dreamed of in your philosophy!"

Notes

1. Harvey Cox, *The Secular City: Secularization and Urbanization in Theological Perspective* (New York: MacMillan, 1965), 20-21. (The book focuses on the increasing effect of secularization and urbanization in society which continues today.)

2. John Robinson, *Honest to God* (SCM Press, 1955).

3. Greta Vosper, *Emerging Cosmology* (1981).

4. Teilard de Chardin, *The Future of Man* (Collins, 1959).

Further Reading

Diamond, Jared M. *The Third Chimpanzee: The Evolution And Future of the Human Animal.* New York: Harper Perennial, 2006. (A light and interesting observation of the genetic growth of the chimpanzee to the human being.)

Edwards, David L. *Religion and Change.* London: Hodder and Stoughton, 1969. (A survey of the influence of the secular in the current world.)

Edwards, David L. *The Future of Christianity.* London: Hodder and Stoughton, 1987. (An analysis of historical, contemporary and future trends within the worldwide church.)

Chapter 2
The Challenge: "There Is No God"

When I was still a teenager I realized that there was no way of proving or explaining the existence of God. Certainly the reality of any kind of *being* outside the physical world could not be proved by science. But, equally strongly, I was convinced that there was much more to human experience than that which could be measured or demonstrated. I have not changed my convictions since then, despite all the challenges that I have encountered throughout my thinking life from those who claim that *God* is merely a figment of my imagination. It is not surprising that I felt challenged to respond to a couple of attacks against this faith which have appeared in print over the last few years. The first of these was the increasingly strong bias which had begun to creep into the press which I read regularly, a bias which has little respect for religion. This has made me sad and I will say no more but a further attack comes from a provocative book by the scientist Richard Dawkins called *The God Delusion.*[1] It was quite clear that Dawkins' intention was not to present just a studied and fresh argument against the Christian religion but a passionate diatribe against religion in all its forms. I have to admit that my own education in science is limited largely to what I learned at school and I must bow to his scientific expertise. However, when he launches into attacking the very concept of believing in the reality of what we call *god*, he has little of real substance to say. He focuses his attacks on two basic things. The first of these is to attack the very concept of god in any shape or form.

There Is No God

It is important to recognize that Dawkins is indeed a first class scientist. The problem lies in the fact that he only sees the world we live in terms of physical science, even things like intuition, feelings and faith. Anything more than that, including the idea of a *Something More* we call *God*, in his understanding, simply doesn't exist. What he is in effect saying is that, since the *physical* is all there *is*, then *God* is *not*. In fact, it is simply a choice that he has made or, if I may put it, an act of faith. This, of course, he is free to do. What disturbs me is the scorn he pours out on those whose faith leads them to another conclusion, that there is indeed more to be said than that which we call the physical, both in our own personal lives and in the world as experienced by us human beings, a *something* we call God, in other words, "You might have faith in a God but I don't!" The fact that he has chosen *not* to believe in any kind of *Something More* does nothing to prove that God does not exist or that the god that many of us believe in is no more than a human fabrication and delusion. Dawkins is guilty of searching for *God* within his own scientific world and then concluding that he isn't there. This is simply tautological. All he is saying is that God's reality cannot be scientifically proven and therefore doesn't exist. He is quite correct in that God may not be scientifically detected, but God may be experienced. The reality is that there are many scientists and critical thinkers in today's world who do not agree with Dawkins. One of these is Alan McGrath, who, like Dawkins, was at Oxford University as a scientist, and who at one time had no faith in a divine being but became a Christian and has written a powerful book challenging Dawkins' publication. As both a scientist and a Christian he has roundly attacked Dawkins' ideas and argued cogently for the reality of God in today's scientific world. Many famous scientists during the last sixty years have and continue to be committed Christians. On another level, many people I have encountered in my own personal life have been both committed Christians and also practicing scientists. One couple is at present working in Cambridge in the field of genetic research, another was involved in the initial development of plastics, many have been practicing in the field of medicine and another is in the field of atomic energy. The list could obviously go on. To think scientifically, most certainly does not mean a denial of the existence of God.

To be fair to Dawkins, I fully accept the fact that he is a scientist who has chosen to see and interpret the world as he sees it solely in a scientific way. He believes that this world as revealed by the scientist is the only world that exists and it follows that, since this is only reality, then any other kind of reality simply does not exist. I would suggest that this stance is as much a matter of faith as that of the Christian. Dawkins has chosen not to believe in the *Something More* we call God but many others, living in this modern scientific world do not agree with him. However, there is more in Dawkins' arguments than a simple statement that there is no God. It is a savage attack not only on the nature of the God revealed in Jesus but also on the Christian Church and it is to these that I now turn. His second attack is to make abusive nonsense of the God of Christianity, even though he has made me smile at his occasional witticisms!

What Is the Nature of this God?

Sadly, Dawkins has chosen to set up a *straw man* of his own concoction which he proceeds to attack vehemently with almost savage delight. The image which he presents is certainly not the God revealed in Jesus nor that which lies at the heart of the Christian faith, which he summarily dismisses when he writes: "Although Jesus probably existed, respectable scholars do not in general regard the New Testament as a reliable record of what happened in history and I shall not consider the bible further as evidence for any kind of deity."[2] In reality, this is simply not true, as I will endeavor to prove later on. Certainly many of the biblical images of the Old Testament illustrate the many ways in which people thought about God during the 2000 years that preceded the coming of Jesus, just as the gods have been portrayed in many other forms of religion. However, it was precisely such primitive images which were attacked by Jesus himself in his own lifetime, images which are very different to those demonstrated in the teaching and person of Jesus.

Dawkins blandly claims that he has "searched the evidence of the Holy Book" effectively as it was written. Poppycock! In reality, he has almost totally ignored the diligent and thorough biblical studies which have been going on for the last hundred years. Dawkins' attack on fundamentalism in Christianity is certainly justified as is the fundamentalism of many other ideologies and faiths. But the vast numbers of Christians are not blind fundamentalists. He seems to be totally ignorant of the remarkable research over the last hundred years, in the fields of both Old and New Testament. This research reveals with great clarity the radical nature of both the life and teachings of Jesus, which present us with a renewed image of God vastly different from that portrayed by Dawkins. He ignores the fresh light shed upon the authenticity of the New Testament and the historical career and teachings of Jesus. The reality is that the most respected scholars of today do in fact believe that the three *synoptic* gospels of Mark, Luke and Matthew really do provide us with relatively accurate accounts of both the life and the teachings of the historical Jesus as well as an equally accurate picture of the early Christian church. It is one of the great breakthroughs of history that scholars are now able to envision and grasp, better than ever before, a true image of the nature of God with regard to each of our own lives and the world of today.

However, it is not only the Bible which is treated in this way by Dawkins. His attack is equally aimed at the Christian church for which he has little good to say. The virulence of his attack on the image of God is also displayed in his scorn directed at the Church's alleged practices. An example of this is his extreme mockery of the Christian rite of Baptism when he writes: "The Catholic Church allowed (and continues to allow) anybody to baptize anybody else. The baptizer doesn't have to be a priest. Neither the child nor the parents, nor anybody else has to consent to the baptism. Nothing needs to be signed. Nothing has to be officially witnessed. All that is necessary is a splash of water, a few words, a helpless child and a superstitious and catechistically brainwashed babysitter."[3] All it needs is a good cartoonist to illustrate it and certainly it provoked a quiet chuckle from me but it is about as far from reality as chalk is from cheese! As Shakespeare put it in Hamlet over four hundred years ago, "Methinks the Lady doth protest too much"; or as David Marshall has pungently observed: "Scientists are human and therefore human sapiens but also sometimes full of hot air!"[4] Dawkins certainly expresses the more extreme views of those who do not believe in any kind of *Something More* other than the world as revealed by today's physical sciences. Yet there are many who wish to hold on to some kind of *religion*, a sense that there is indeed *Something More* than the strictly scientific. So far, I have focused on the blatant attack of Dawkins upon the reality of any kind of deity, especially the god of Christianity and his assumption that god cannot be proved by physical science and therefore cannot exist. It all sounds cut and dry but is it as simple as that?

The God of the Atom

As I have pointed out, there are a growing number of people in the scientific community who believe that God is *not* in fact *dead* and that scientific studies point increasingly to the reality of a *Something More* which is indeed *outside* the physical world and which we have traditionally called *God*. In the world that immediately followed Charles Darwin and way into our own times, it was broadly assumed that *evolution* meant simply that there was no god, nor was there any need for such a concept. It was assumed that human life simply evolved as part of the overall evolutionary system. God came slowly to be seen as redundant and wholly unnecessary in the eyes of the scientific community, leading to the all-round assumption that there was simply no God. However, many scientists in today's world are now beginning to admit that there is indeed *Something More* other than the purely physical. One of these is Michael Behe, a respected biochemist and intelligent design advocate scientist working in the field of the most basic and minute elements of the world we live in. Without going into the complexities of his research, I will endeavour to summarize some of his basic conclusions. In his book *Darwin's Black Box*[5] Behe takes us down to the most simple and basic forms of life on our planet, the micro world of molecules, proteins and cells, the very building blocks of all life on the planet. He outlines the immense complexity of the changes which have taken place in the micro world since its very beginning. He explains the immense complexity of these changes and developments which have taken place in the process of evolution, from the tiniest of basic cells to the beginnings of human life, and points to "the unbridgeable chasms that occur even at the tiniest levels of life," let alone in the later incredible complexion called "complex theory," which he says "cannot explain the origins of the complex biochemical structures that make for life" to which he adds the words: "it doesn't even try!" Ultimately, he comes to the conclusion that "the influence of design can be held with all the firmness that is possible in this world without knowing anything of the designer." All of this, he claims, leads him and many other scientists to the conclusion that science is indeed pointing to the element of design in the evolutionary process and that such design inevitably demands a designer. He even goes further when he speaks not only of design but of evidence of *intelligent* design or what the great thinker Paul Tillich once described as "the ground of future possibility as well as being the ground of order and intelligibility" as well as "the ground of our being," a constant theme of his book *Systematic Theology*.[6]

There are indeed many others within the scientific field who fully agree with such conclusions and are powerful in their claim that the findings of scientific research in the field of the evolution, from the smallest particles to today's human life, point to the reality of the *Something More* which we call *God*, a reality to which a growing number of scientists in today's scientific community would agree.

God of the Universe

A second example is that of Diarmuid O'Murchu, a social psychologist who is an advocate of *intelligent design* and is also a priest and whose book *Quantum Theology*[7] focuses on the implications of the *New Physics* of today. In his book, he is trying to grapple with the meaning of *God* in the vast universe that embraces us. In essence, his answer is that God is within the very process of evolution in both our own world and the developing universe in all its immensity. In fact, it is what Christians have traditionally called *immanent* (i.e. *within* the system rather than outside it.) He calls God "the creative energy which survives and grows amid the continuous flow and change, complexity and design" (Chap VII). He defines this vision as "a continual cooperation within our own evolving universe leading us to a fresh horizon of wholeness, hope and possibility." Even though this leads him into a possible denial of what traditional theology has called the *transcendence* of God (i.e. that God is totally outside the physical world) he is pointing us to the powerful reality of God in our physical world, the world we live in. This is what theologians call the *immanence* of the divine, the God *in our midst*. In this sense, O'Murchu focuses on God in our world, in the process of "universal development and change," a god we can experience and to whom we can pray as living persons. He gives new meaning to what is implied by the words of Jesus when he spoke of the "Kingdom of God," a meaning which opens us to a new vision of the world as God would have it to be. O'Murchu is passionately pointing out that God is very much *in* our world when he says very powerfully: "God is not a passive and external ruler but a passionate, relational presence embodied in the creative, evolutionary process itself" as a result of which "our world will become a new place where we choose to take love seriously" and "that there is a fundamental unity to our universe transcending all our divisions and distinctions developed in our human world." What these two scientists bring to our attention is that God is in creation, in its tiniest atoms and in the "vast expanse of interstellar space."[8] There is a process which is ongoing and of which God is the creator. Perhaps most importantly of all in the world and society we live in day by day, it points to the vision which God has given us, of a world not only of enormous complexity but also of hope, faith and compassion and of a *Something More* whom we can each come to know and experience on our individual journeys. It is this God on which we shall be focusing from now onwards.

Notes

1. Richard Dawkins, *The God Delusion* (Houghton Mifflin 2006).

2. Dawkins, *The God Delusion*, 97.

3. Dawkins, *The God Delusion*, 312.

4. David Marshall, *The Truth Behind the New Atheism: Responding to the Emerging Challenges to God and Christianity* (Eugene: Harvest House Publishers, 2007).

5. Michael J. Behe, *Darwin's Black Box: The Biochemical Challenge to Evolution.* (New York: The Free Press, 1996).

6. Paul Tilllich, *Systematic Theology* (London: Nisbet, 1951).

7. Diarmuid O'Murchu, *Quantum Theology: Spiritual Implications of the New Physics* (New York: Crossroad, 2004), See Chapter VII.

8. *Anglican Book of Alternative Services* (Anglican Book Centre, 1983).

Further Reading

Armstrong, Karen. *A History of God: The 4,000-Year Quest of Judaism, Christianity, and Islam.* New York: Ballantine Books, 1993.

Grayling, A.C. *The Reason of Things.* London: Phoenix, 2003.

Horgan, John. *The End of Science: Facing the Limits of Knowledge in the Twilight of the Scientific Age.* New York: Broadway Books, 1997.

Keller, Timothy. *The Reason for God: Belief in an Age of Skepticism.* New York: Dutton, 2008.

Marshall, David. *The Truth Behind the New Atheism: Responding to the Emerging Challenges to God and Christianity.* Eugene: Harvest House Publishers, 2007 (A challenging comment on today's atheism and its effects on Christian faith.)

McGrath, Alister. Intellectuals Don't Need God & Other Modern Myths: Building Bridges to Faith Through Apologetics. Grand Rapids: Zondervan Publishing House, 1993.

O'Murchu, Diarmuid. Quantum Theology: Spiritual Implications of the New Physics (New York: Crossroad, 2004) (An understanding that God is not so much up there but is a presence in the world we live in i.e. "immanent rather than transcendent.")

Polkinghorne, John. *The Way the World is: The Christian Perspective of a Scientist.* Louisville: Westminster John Knox Press, 2007.

Chapter 3
Is the Bible True?

The Results of Biblical Criticism

If we are truly convinced that there is indeed a *Something More*, we are faced with another question. Just what is the nature of this God? How can we define and experience this god? The response of the early Christians to these questions is to be found in the historical person of a man called Jesus in whom they sensed this divine presence, a revelation of God, which lead them to refer to Jesus as the Son of God. Through him, it is clear that their own lives were radically transformed and they were led to a vision of a renewed world which they called the Kingdom of God.

The account of all this is to be found in the New Testament of the Bible and this leads us to another question. Are their accounts of the life and teachings of this man Jesus historically accurate and, even if all of them are not literally so, just what *do* they reveal that we can accept as true? Did Jesus really heal people as the Gospels tell us? Did he really say all the things that are written in them? How come that they don't all agree? Just how accurate are those Gospels and how much is it really possible to get through to the real *historical* Jesus?

Such questions as these are exactly what Biblical scholars throughout the world have been striving to answer over the last hundred years. Just what have they been doing and what are the fruits of their labours? In what follows I will be focusing upon the works of various contemporary theologians in their attempts to respond to these questions so that we may have a clearer picture of the historical Jesus and what he was doing and teaching in the Palestine of 2000 years ago.

The Impact of Biblical Criticism

Until relatively late in the nineteenth century, most people's understanding and way of looking at the bible was what we would now call *fundamentalist*. At its simplest, this word implies that it was totally written by the hand of God both in the Old and New Testaments, including, of course, all of what Jesus did and said. The breakout from this very basic way of thinking came about through the results of Biblical Criticism, which radically changed the hitherto literal interpretation of the Bible in all its totality. The new way came as a shock wave to those of a more traditional way of thinking about both the Old and New Testaments. Many people today continue to see both of these as literally having been dictated by direct word of God and taken at their literal value. For those whose faith is based on this interpretation I have simply to say that it is their choice to which they are entitled. However, most people within the Church do not hold this opinion and it is to these that I direct all that follows. Today, many of us ask ourselves, "Just what is the historical truth in the Bible whether it be the Old or the New Testament? Just how much can we trust it? Just what kind of *truth* are we talking about? How much of what is written about is historically accurate, how much is legend, how much metaphor, how much is simply reflecting the cultures of two millennia ago?" These are difficult questions which Biblical scholars have been wrestling with for well over a century and it is to these that I address the rest of this chapter.

The Old Testament

The work of scholars of the Old Testament and in archaeological research has opened up a vast new understanding of its contents. It reveals what is in fact a rich library of literature of all kinds ranging from poetry, myth, legend, dreams, court documents, wise sayings, sermons and many more as well as what we might call *history*, even though the precise accuracy of the last cannot always be taken literally. In saying this, I do not mean to denigrate such history for what it is (i.e. a rich record of the experiences of a people called the Jews and their special relationship they had with their God whom they called *Yahweh.*) I will not attempt to go into the even broader details of that epic story which would take up volumes on its own but I will attempt a brief reference to the studies that have taken place over the last sixty years. Some of the most important studies have been in the field of archaeology which has provided much material evidence both backing up and questioning the accuracy of the many historical events recorded in the Bible. Hershel Shanks, at one time editor of the *American Biblical and Archaeological Journal* and William Deaver of the University of Arizona, together with a significant number of other experts in this field have had great influence in opening up our understanding of the history of the Holy Land and it does not end there. Studies have combined in presenting us with a clear understanding of the history of the people of Israel and their neighbours which has led especially to a far deeper perception of how the contents of the New Testament came to be written and how they are to be interpreted today.

The dramatic discovery in 1949 of the Dead Sea Scrolls caught the attention of the world in bringing to light a critical point in the history of both Jews and Christians, even though it raised new questions. The scrolls contained the remnants of writings of what was probably a Jewish sect (somewhat like a monastery) which was destroyed by the Romans in about 60 AD. The scrolls themselves were probably the contents of a library containing references and documents which suggested possible links to the new Christian sect, then in its infancy. The discovery led to a flurry of academic research by such scholars as Robert Eiseman, Hershel Shanks and Norman Golg, (see *Further Reading*) as well as others from the Jewish community. While these documents are not a part of the Bible, they continue to shed important light on possible links between Christians and Jews during those very formative days of the Christian movement, to which I now turn.

New Testament Criticism
Its Roots and Influence

The critical approach to the New Testament began in the first part of the twentieth century and it came as a shock to those of a more traditional way of thinking, particularly when it comes to the accounts of Jesus. It raised many challenging questions. Were all the recorded stories of Jesus, his birth and life, his journeys and activities, his sayings and miracles not really true? Did his healings actually take place? Did he really feed several thousand people with just five barley loaves? Did he really raise Lazarus from the dead? Are the exchanges he had with the Pharisees and Sadducees all accurate, word for word? Did he really turn a tub of water into wine? How accurate are the accounts of his trial and execution? And, most importantly, did he really reappear to his followers after his death? And what of all his sayings? Are they to be treated as if they had been recorded on a tape? And how is it that all four gospels do not agree, especially that of John? Just how accurate are the gospels? All of these lead to the challenging question, "If they are not literally true, then just what *was* true? To what truths did all of these things point?" It is questions such as these that came to be raised during the late nineteenth century, not only by experts but by many who were sitting in the church pews.

During the last few decades, an increasing amount of new historical material has begun to emerge. A hitherto new *Gospel of Thomas* was discovered which differed quite radically from those existing in New Testament and which portrayed Jesus in quite a different way from the other four gospels. One interesting difference is that it was written in Aramaic, the language of Jesus, rather than the Greek of the traditional gospels. There was also the discovery of some very early Christian texts in a desert place called Nag Hagadi, a version which shed light on the thinking of some very early Christians in Egypt, again showing differences from the writings of the four gospels. All of this provided additional material to help us respond to the questions which I have already listed.

All that I have just been describing has been the subject of so-called *Biblical Criticism* which has been taking place over the last sixty or so years. One of its earliest figures is that of the German scholar Martin Bultmann (1884-1976) who set about distinguishing between "things as they really were" through a process he called "Form Criticism" and applying this to the Bible, especially the New Testament. Did Jesus really do and say exactly what was recorded in the gospel texts? Just what was historically true and what was pure myth? To get at this, he laid out the four gospels, alongside each other in order to compare them. He pointed out just how different they were and he suggested why. In this way, he and an increasing number of others set about discovering how each of them came to be written and how they also frequently related to each other in many ways. Out of all these growing studies, it was established that, of the four gospels, that of Mark was clearly the earliest. It was agreed that Luke and Matthew had each used Mark's writings as their base texts and how the Gospel of John was written much later. One significant conclusion was that John is very different to the other three. It was not only written later but was much more *theological* than the others. No doubt John had had longer to think and ponder about just what the events of Jesus' life and reappearances were all about and to put his own *spin* upon it. As the critics continued their studies, it became increasingly clear just how the gospels had developed. This is particularly true about just when and in what ways their contents are distinguishable between *actual history* and the writers' own interpretation.

I have already mentioned the name of Martin Bultmann but I would also like to add the contributions of many others who, during later years, have developed his earlier work. Two of my own teachers when I was at Cambridge in the 50's were Charles Moule and John Robinson, both of them very much a part of this movement. The latter became a household name in England with the production of his bestseller called *Honest to God* (1955) a book which opened the eyes of many people and caused a significant shock wave in the popular press. In America, Richard Fuller of Seaman Western University wrote a book called *The Foundations of Christology* (1965) in which he attempted to reveal the continuity between the "historical Jesus" and the later message and witness of the post-resurrection church. In other words, what Jesus *actually* did and said as opposed to how the disciples understood them. Since then, the work of the critics has continued. The *God is Dead* movement has somewhat lost its thread and interest has moved in a more positive direction. Instead of being seen by many as a threat to the traditional understanding of Jesus and his message, it has moved into a more positive understanding of what is really at the core of the Christian faith. In practical terms this has led to a deeper grasp of the historic role and teaching of Jesus and his followers and their impact of these on each one of us and our world of today. One landmark was the publication of the *Five*

Gospels in 1993, which was a search for the authentic words of Jesus by Robert W. Funk and others. It caught the public attention and became almost a benchmark. It has left us with a clearer image of the actual person of Jesus and a clearer understanding of what he was specifically doing and saying in the brief time he was with us. Two contemporary writers have been particularly adept at developing the positive results of all these studies in such a way that they make sense and provide clarity to readers at all levels. They are the Roman Catholic Dominic Crossan of St. Paul's University in Chicago and Marcus Borg, a Lutheran theologian from the United States (see *Further Reading*). Both of them have contributed series of significant books which combine scholarly depth with public appeal. Marcus Borg's writing has been described by one his critics as "a revisiting of Christianity's heart and soul."

Conclusion

What then has been learned as a result of all these studies over the last few decades? Just what are we to believe as we read the contents of both the Old and, even more, of the New Testament? In what way do we now have a more accurate picture of the life and teaching of Jesus and their relevance to the world in which we live today? I believe that these studies have indeed led us to new insights into the experiences of those first followers of Jesus, especially regarding what kind of a person he was and what was at the heart of his words and actions. Even more deeply, they have given us a renewed insight into the reality and nature of the *Something More* we call God. Both of these we shall further explore. What it also does is to make nonsense of the basic assumptions of Dawkins that the New Testament especially is no more than a concoction of a bunch of deluded fanatics.

To sum up, what has come out of all this deepening understanding of the small library we call the New Testament? I believe that the last few decades have witnessed the continuing acceptance by the Christian community of two things: firstly the acceptance of the historic reality of Jesus, that is, the human person whose presence was experienced by his followers, not only in the days before his execution but in the following weeks; secondly an acceptance that his followers continued to experience that presence in the years that followed, leading them to call him the Son of God. They carried with them a vision which they believed was of God, a vision given to them through both the life and teaching of Jesus.

Further Reading for Chapters Three and Four

Amongst the following books below, I would especially encourage readers to delve into a series of books written by three particular authors*, working both individually and together. Marcus Borg, a Lutheran, has a gift as a New Testament scholar and has collaborated with Tom Wright, an Anglican, and Dominic Crossan, a Roman Catholic; all of them highly respected scholars.

Armstrong, David, ed. *The Truth About Jesus.* Grand Rapids: Eerdmans, 1998.

*Borg, Marcus J. Jesus in Contemporary Scholarship. Valley Forge: Trinity Press International, 1994.

Borg, Marcus J. Jesus: Uncovering the Life, Teachings, and Relevance of a Religious Revolutionary. San Francisco: Harper, 2006.

Borg, Marcus J., and *N. T. Wright. *The Meaning of Jesus: Two Visions.* San Francisco: Harper, 1999.

Caird, C.B. The Apostolic Age. London: Duckworth, 1955.

*Crossan, Dominic. The Birth of Christianity: Discovering What Happened in the Years Immediately After the Execution of Jesus. San Francisco: Harper, 1998.

Dunn, James D.G. The Evidence for Jesus. London: S.C.M., 1998.

Eisenman, Robert. The Dead Sea Scrolls and the First Christians: Essays and Translations. Edison: Castle Books, 2004.

Freyne, Sean. *Galilee, Jesus and the Gospels: Literary Approaches and Historical Investigations.* Philadelphia: Fortress Press, 1988.

Funk, Robert W. *The Five Gospels.* Santa Rosa: Polebridge Press, 1993.

Golb, Norman. Who Wrote the Dead Sea Scrolls?: The Search for the Secret of Qumran. New York: Scribener, 1995.

Robinson, John A.T. Can We Trust the New Testament? Grand Rapids: Eerdmans, 1977.

Shanks, Hershel. *Understanding the Dead Sea Scrolls: A Reader from the Biblical Archaeology Review.* New York: Random House, 1992.

Theissen, Gerd. *Sociology of Early Palestinian Christianity.* Philadelphia: Fortress Press, 1978. (Focus on the fact that Jesus spent most of his life in the countryside of Galilee of his time.)

Theissen, Gerd. *The Shadow of the Galilean.* Philadelphia: Fortress Press, 1978.

Vermes, Geza. *Jesus the Jew.* Philadelphia : Fortress Press, 1992.

Vermes, Geza. *The Religion of Jesus the Jew.* Minneapolis: Fortress Press, 1993.

Chapter 4
The Jesus of History

As I have previously pointed out, the intense work of biblical scholars has shed fresh light on the writings of the New Testament, particularly in the four canonical gospels. This has been especially true when it comes to dealing with the historical accuracy of both the events in the life of Jesus and of his many sayings and actions. It has also helped us to get a firmer grasp on what we would now call the *spin*, as his early followers tried to explain all that they had seen and heard. Those who recorded his words and actions clearly did not go around equipped with microphones and cameras. Jesus did not have a personal secretary who recorded what he said and did. Just how literally accurate, then, were the texts which we now read in today's New Testament? We are left with two options: we can take it all literally, including all the *spin* which the writers inevitably included; or try to get back more precisely to what actually happened.

Just who was this *Jesus*, who was to change the course of history some 2000 years ago? As a result of all the studies of the past century, just what do we know of this man? Just what is clear after all these years of research and scholarship? What kind of a person was he? What exactly happened over those three or so years of publicity and what were his teaching and actions all about? He was certainly a convincing and inspiring leader of both men and women. He was a powerful story teller who had a deep grasp of human personality. He could argue head to head with the teachers of his day and had a lofty vision of a new way of living and, indeed, of a new world. But this was not all. He undeniably had an amazing gift of healing, demonstrated repeatedly during his travels about the country. He was also seen as a *man of God* in the style of the old Hebrew prophets and, like them, sharply challenged the rich and the powerful of the land—a challenge which ultimately led to his execution. He also attracted a band of faithful followers who came to be called his Disciples, embracing both men and women from both the countryside and the cities, people who were drawn to him by his charisma and teaching. Many began to see him as the new Messiah, a leader who would overthrow the Roman occupation and restore Israel to its former glory. Not everyone that he encountered welcomed him. In Nazareth, he was forcibly dragged from the local synagogue and only just escaped being cast from a nearby precipice. He was powerful in his challenge to the rich and powerful in society, not only to the wealthy landlords and the bankers and moneylenders of his day but also to the religious leaders many of whom misused their power as a means of enriching themselves while lauding it over others. Above all, he had deep concern for the sick, the poor and the victims and *have-nots* in his society. Inevitably, the authorities had more than enough from this rabble-rouser whose teachings and activities had become a serious threat to both the Jewish hierarchy and the occupying military forces of the Roman Empire. After a brief trial before both Priestly and Roman courts, he was duly executed, together with a couple of thieves and the leaders of both the Jewish Temple and the Roman army of occupation who no doubt gave sighs of relief. It was one more terrorist out of the way. But, to his closest followers, it was a disaster and the dead body of Jesus was put safely away in the tomb of a friend.

At this point, the followers of Jesus probably thought it was end of the story, the story of an amazing man who, much like the prophets before him, had been inspired by the Spirit of God. Some of his followers later even suffered or were put to death for what they did and said. Here was another holy man, a man of God, a man in whom they had sensed the presence of the divine, the presence of God. At his death and burial, they mourned in sorrow and despair. Before this, there had been intimations of the *Something More* shown throughout three years of his ministry. During that time they had witnessed some amazing things that had happened, quite apart from his powerful teachings. In it all many of them had experienced a *numinous* presence of the divine but now it had come to a disastrous end as the broken body of Jesus was put away in the tomb. Then something happened which was to change everything. The memories recorded in the New Testament clearly relate how Jesus had re-appeared after his execution, not once but several times and to many people. What actually happened at this point is somewhat confusing. The precise details continue to be debated by the critics who will probably never entirely agree but what is abundantly clear is that the reality and experience of these reappearances changed the lives of those who had been timid and frightened followers of Jesus into bold and spirit filled people eager to spread the gospel, or good news, about Jesus.

The familiar account in the Gospels of Jesus' life, including his re-appearance, is now accepted as a series of historical events which few if any would question. It is now accepted by the majority of theologians, as the historical, if not always chronological, record of the events which actually took place 2000 years ago. They actually happened and were real. Despair was turned into hope and what we now call the Christian faith began to take root and grew. Scholars have continued to reflect on just what had been happening in those dramatic three years and throughout those that followed.

Note. For those who wish to go more deeply into the specific details, I would strongly suggest that they study a review of this by the contemporary New Testament critic Marcus Borg, whose book *Jesus, the Life, Teaching and*

Relevance of a Religious Revolutionary I have found immensely clear and cogent.

Just what is the Core of Truth?—Yes, God is Real

Before continuing, I will digress for a moment. Throughout human history, men and women have believed in the reality of the *Something More* we call God, that there was and is more to reality than the physical world we live in. It has been called by many names, from the *holy*, the *divine* or simply *God*. The Protestant theologian Rudolph Otto (1869-1937) in his widely acclaimed book *The Idea of the Holy* referred to it as the *numinous*, which he described in the Latin words *mysterium, tremendum et fascinans,* a sense of awe, mystery and religious fascination.

Despite the rejection of such a reality by critics like Richard Dawkins and even Gretta Vosper, the vast number of people in our world continues to believe in this *Something More* which lies at the very heart of all religious belief. The Christian faith is based upon the experience of those early Christian followers of Jesus some 2000 years ago and of the records they left behind them in the New Testament. These biblical records have been confirmed and clarified for us as a result of positive critical studies. At the very core of these there is a general agreement that "God was in Christ, reconciling the world to himself." It is clear that these words imply that *Something More* was evident in the life of Jesus. He was seen as a man who was deeply endued with the presence of God and revealed not only the reality of God but also what God was like, just what was God's *nature*. In what follows now is my understanding of the generally agreed results of the biblical scholarship over the last hundred or so years

The Core of the Gospel As Revealed in Jesus

We are going to be looking at a number of important events which are historically recorded in the life of Jesus. Together they point to both the reality and the nature of God, especially in what I call the *numinous* events which his followers experienced. We find these events in both the life of Jesus as recorded in the Gospels, and further clarified by all the research which has taken place over the last century. To go through all the evidence would take far too long but, in what follows, I will refer to some of the most notable episodes.

The first is the account of the baptism of Jesus by a man called John and recorded in the Gospel of Mark (1.9-12). It describes the very beginning of the ministry of Jesus. It was a moment when he appeared in public for the first time as something more than just a peasant from the countryside. The record describes how a man called John was baptizing numbers of people in the waters of the River Jordan. The symbol of washing John's followers with water was a symbol of their enrolment into a group of what we would probably call *radicals* in our own day. The record describes that, as the baptism of Jesus took place, all who were standing by shared in an awesome experience. John himself is said to have had a vision in which he sensed the presence of the numinous in this unknown young man and sees him as a particularly *holy* person. It revealed to him the person of Jesus as a new prophet, a charismatic leader who would lead God's people. It was in that life changing experience that Jesus is said to have discovered his calling and, from then onward, the people began to follow him as they saw, in him, the awesome presence of the *Something More*. It marked the beginning of the ministry of Jesus, a man who had no doubt always been spiritually conscious of God but, for whom from that moment, it had attained a new intensity and purpose. Something was experienced by all who were there and who were witnessing the beginning of the movement which was to change their lives. It was from this point that Jesus stepped into the public limelight and was openly recognized as being one who was filled with and inspired with the presence of God. Today, perhaps, he might have been called some kind of charismatic, although it was far deeper and more powerful than that. It was indeed a unique moment which began to open the eyes of his followers to the reality of God present in Jesus.

Somewhat later, his *divine* character is also displayed in another awesome account of a powerful vision which was experienced by a small number of his followers which came to be called the *Transfiguration*, a strange vision which Mark included in his gospel. In it, he relates how a small number of Jesus' disciples had a vision of Jesus together with two of the most revered Old Testament figures, Elijah and Moses. Mark recounts how the disciples heard a voice saying: "This is my son, hear him," after which the vision vanished. This was no usual sighting. It was a vision, something which I myself have experienced. It was not something that could be relayed on a TV screen but it *was something* that happened. It was a real experience shared by those who were there, an experience which carries an important message. I fully realize that such a vision cannot of itself prove the existence of God in the scientific terms which Dawkins demands but it does emphasize the reality experienced by those followers on that mountain 2000 years ago, the reality of the *Something More* revealed in the person of Jesus.

If many would hesitate in regarding the above two episodes as solid examples of the reality of the divine, it is impossible to deny some experiences that were far more down to earth. Certainly the most convincing of all the episodes in Jesus' life had to do, not so much with such visions but with his much more down to earth actions amongst the people who were increasingly drawn to him over the three years of his ministry wherever he went across the country. I am talking about the much recorded acts of *healing* which must have been witnessed, not just by his immediate followers, but by huge numbers of bystanders. These healings were experienced by real people who were *made whole*. I will select just a few. One tells the story of two blind men who came up to Jesus asking him to heal them to which Jesus replied, "Do you believe that I am able to do this?" To which they replied, "Yes Lord." We are then told that Jesus touched their eyes, and they were opened (Matthew 9.27-31).

Mark, in his gospel, tells of a similar story when he recounts the healing of a blind man in the village of Bethesda, one which is more specific. He recounts how the man came up to Jesus and begged him to touch him. The story continues to tell how Jesus spat on his eyes and laid his hands on him, asking him if he could see anything. The man said, "I see men but they seem like trees walking," after which Jesus again laid his hands on him and, this time, the man saw clearly. (Mark 10.22-26) Another story tells of how a boy was healed of his epilepsy. He had been in the habit of foaming at the mouth and grinding his teeth as well as casting himself into both fire and water. His father brought him to Jesus and asked him to heal his son. Jesus prayed. The story tells how the child at first cried out and went into a convulsion before collapsing, so that those around him thought that he was dead. But, as Mark recounts, "Jesus took him up by the hand and lifted him up, and he arose." (Mark 9.14-29). These are just a few of the amazing number of accounts which we find in the records of the Gospel writers in which we sense the presence of the *Something More* which the people of his time saw in the person of Jesus. There is no possible doubt that these and the many more healings actually happened that they were what Rudolph Otto called the *numinous*, the presence of God and the reality of the Divine. They were evidence of God somehow present and working in the person of Jesus. We are not talking here of neat stories of Jesus as a little boy making pretty birds out of the mud around his house, (as recorded in some later legend of his life). Nor are we accepting the literal accuracy of all the legends surrounding his birth, such as the arrival of the kings and the gifts of the shepherds, which are recognized by nearly all critics as additions added on later to substantiate the significance of Jesus' life. What we are talking about are the agreed historical facts of his ministry, all of which point to the reality of the *Something More* revealed in the person of Jesus, a God whom others so callously throw out of the window.

Yet there was more to come. In the years immediately following the execution of Jesus we read the dramatic accounts of his re-appearance to his followers, which were to trigger the birth of a new religion called *Christianity*. But just what really did happen? Did Jesus really appear again after his death and burial? What were the hard events recorded in the somewhat confusing records of the Gospels? Just what are the findings of the basic critical studies over the last sixty years? The answers are in fact quite clear. According to the New Testament, what happened was a series of occasions when a significant number of the disciples actually saw and heard him again after his execution and burial. The accounts tell how they saw him again with their eyes and heard him address them.

It is on the veracity of these experiences that many of them were later to be ready to even surrender their lives. In the years immediately following the death and re-appearance of Jesus, his followers continued to experience the reality of this *Something More* which they called the *Holy Spirit*, a reality displayed not only in their individual lives but in the growing communities of Christians which grew up to become the Church, a reality which continues to this day and which lies at the very heart of the Christian faith. Yes Mr. Dawkins, there is indeed a God. This certainly does leave us with another question, "Just what kind of God?"

I will pause here in order to touch on the image of God which had preceded the coming of Jesus and which we find in the writings of the Old Testament. This is a vitally important question to ask in the light of the fact that people over the ages have imagined god (or the gods) in all kinds of ways, from the tribal deities of primitive man, to the more sophisticated gods of the Greeks and Romans, the Yahweh of the Jewish peoples, the Allah of the Islam faith, the deities of the Hindu faith and many more. In these and more, God has been portrayed in many different ways. One of them is the image we find in the Old Testament of the Bible, which has played a powerful part in molding the faith of many Christian followers into our own day, especially those who see the Old Testament as the literal words of God. It is the image of a God who is vengeful and demands retribution for all of our sins. The fact is that the library which we call the Old Testament reflects the images of God held by the Hebrew people over a very large period of time during which the conceptions of God changed and varied from the angry god of the tribes escaping from the Egyptians and establishing themselves in a new land, to the more sophisticated images of the prophets and many later writers. In the Judaism of Jesus' time, religion was expressed in a vast number of laws which had to be strictly obeyed by all. Strict laws precisely defined every moment of each person's life and also the government and corporate life of the nation. As well as these laws, it also included the offerings of animals and other sacrifices at the Temple in Jerusalem in order to *atone* for all the rules that had been broken, a practice that provided substantial profits to those who made money out of the sacrifices. God was very much one who must be obeyed or one must face vengeance. The laws were multitudinous and touched on virtually every action of daily life and its keeping was guarded by a vast hierarchy of officials exercising considerable power over people's lives. God was seen as the ultimate judge whose power was overriding. This was the image seen through the eyes of the people, a picture that Jesus was to challenge. It was an image that he was to replace with a new vision of the *heart* of God.

The God Revealed in Jesus

What, then, is the image of God as revealed in the life and teachings of Jesus, a life which was witnessed by those first followers of his and gave them insight into the true nature of God? I have already cited several instances which revealed the reality of the God in the life of Jesus long before what his follows termed the Resurrection. Perhaps the most resounding was the deep and fundamental love which he displayed to people and reveals what is at the very heart of God's nature. This image of a loving and compassionate God continues to resonate continually in his ministry. It is to be seen in the story of a woman who had been suffering from a flow of blood for many years. (Mark 5.24-34) She was a part of a large crowd of people seeking healing and pressing around Jesus. She said that if only she could touch the hem of Jesus' garment she would be healed. This she did and the flow of blood was instantly stopped but immediately Jesus turned around "feeling the power go out of him" and asked who touched him. When the woman admitted that it was she Jesus said, "Go on your way, your faith has made you whole." It was both simple and dramatic and it suggested yet another element in what happened. It was that, in approaching Jesus, the woman was in fact opening herself to God, as a result of which he was healed, or *made whole*. Similarly there is the story told of the healing of Jairus' daughter. (Mark 5.22, 35-43) Jairus was a ruler of the local Synagogue whose daughter was very sick. He asked Jesus to go and lay his hands on his daughter and she would be healed. As Jesus arrived at the house he was told that it was too late the girl had died. Jesus however told them not to be afraid but to believe. He took only the girl's parents and three disciples with him into the room where the girl was lying. Taking the little girl by the hand he told her to get up, which she did to the amazement of everyone. There are many more tales of such healings. Mark's gospel relates an account of the healing of a leper, the next most frightening of all ancient diseases. With a quiet touch of his hand and a few simple words, the man's leprosy vanishes and, in spite of Jesus' request, the man is not able to contain his joy in telling everyone he met what had happened. (Mark 2.42-44) On another occasion, early in Jesus' ministry, he was confronted by a large crowd outside the home where he was staying and four men appeared, carrying with them a paralyzed man. When they couldn't break through the crowds, they forced a way in through the roof of the house and let the man down. We are told how Jesus, "seeing their faith" and after a shoving match with some protesters healed the man who then stood up and faced the crowd. Quite an event! The list of such healings goes on at great length, covering all kinds of diseases and illnesses. Often people had to line up in order to be healed. Whatever else one may say about Jesus, there is no doubt that these events and many like them really happened. The question again is what do they reveal about the nature of God? This is not surely the angry and testy god of the Old Testament; a god who would probably have been seen as causing all the diseases I have been describing, a god of wrath and judgment. Rather, what we are seeing displayed is a revelation of the true nature of God, a God of infinite love and compassion, revealed in the many healings that highlighted Jesus' whole ministry.

I turn now to that element of Jesus' life and teaching which was perhaps the most compelling of all. I am referring to the sayings and especially the *parables* which peppered the three years of his ministry and which had such a powerful effect on the people of his times, inspiring those who had "ears to hear" what he was saying but also provoking those who didn't like it at all. I will share a number of these and then summarize what they have to teach us today.

One such parable was that of the *Great Supper* (Luke 14.15-24) when Jesus tells the story of a rich employer who gave a great banquet for all his wealthy friends but, by the time for it came, all of them, one by one, had turned down the invitation with different excuses. They were all too busy. So the man told his servant to go out into the streets of the city and bring in all the poor and the maimed, the blind and the lame. All were invited and, no doubt, they all had a great time. But the sting came at the end when the rich man said, "None of those invited (presumably those who had not turned up) shall taste of my banquet!" The societal undertone of this was inescapable. A similar twist is expressed in a story told of a rich young man who came up to Jesus and asked him how he could inherit eternal life, to which Jesus replied that he should "sell all that he had and distribute it to the poor." Then, when the young man had sadly turned away, Jesus remarked: "how hard it will be for a rich man to enter the Kingdom of Heaven." (Luke 16.19-34).

To change to Jesus' actions for a brief moment we need to contrast that last parable with an event which happened when Jesus was traveling towards Jerusalem. (Luke 19.1-9). We read of a man named Zaccheus who was a tax-collector and like most of his kin, was not liked by most people although the job was certainly well-paying. The heart of this hard man was deeply touched when Jesus the wandering teacher asked him, a despised tax collector, if he could stay with him for the night. Zaccheus' immediate response to hearing this surprising request was amazing. It was to give away half of his riches to repay all the profits he had taken from people in the course of his trade. God is revealed in Jesus as a God, not only of compassion but as a god who challenges us to do justice in the world, about which there is more later.

Perhaps the best known of all Jesus' parables is that of *The Good Samaritan*, a story which today leaves most of us feeling warm and comfortable when we read of the kindness that was shown to a man left lying by the roadside after having been attacked and robbed of all his goods. The parable goes on to describe how first a rabbi and then a Jewish teacher ignored the injured man and left him lying in the gutter. They didn't want to get involved or to break the law by getting their hands ritually dirty. So they ignored the injured man and passed him by, leaving him in the gutter. But then along came a Samaritan, (the Samaritans were group of people despised by the Jews of the day,) who took pity on him, took care of his wounds and then took him to the nearest inn and paid for him to stay there until he was better. The message of the parable was clear: not just a nice story but a clarion cry that God's love is able to reach out to all people and not only from those who regard themselves as his *chosen few*. It was not only a nice story but a new vision of human society and of the world as God would have it. It was, in fact, a very *political* statement and would have been seen by many as a threat to the society of their day. To the correct Jew of his time, to be a Samaritan would be regarded as an outsider, unclean, not one of *us*, someone who was different and not a true and accepted Jew. Jesus was here attacking those who lived by the strict purity laws rather than showing compassion to a fellow human being. According to the purity laws those passers-by would have made themselves unclean by touching the injured man. It was also implying that there was a place for all people, not just the chosen few, in God's *Kingdom*, a Kingdom not so much *up there* as *down here* in the world we live in, a world as God would have it. To sum up, what we see running throughout the actions and sayings of Jesus is a deep insight into the reality of a God of infinite compassion and justice, two words which continue to have enormous relevance and importance, as I will indicate in my final chapters.

The Reappearance of Jesus

Finally of course, we reach the climax which lies at the heart of the Christian gospel and constitutes the very core of the Christian faith. I am, of course, referring to the final scenes of Jesus' life as it was witnessed by those who followed him, his death and his re-appearance. These events are now accepted by the vast number of critics as history which actually happened. Few today would argue that Jesus really was executed by crucifixion and that his body was actually buried just outside the old walls of Jerusalem. About this, clearly there is no argument.

It is also true to say that, soon after this event, a significant number of his followers claimed to have seen him, listen to and spoken with him, touched him and eaten with him. It is impossible to *prove* this by scientific means. The only people who were there were all his followers. Neither Dawkins nor any others like him were there to prove or disprove his existence scientifically and the evidence of his appearances is there for us today to take or leave. It is up to each one of us to make our own decision to believe the evidence as we have received it or not. I will, then, leave us with a summary of what I believe the scholars have learned about the nature of this God as revealed by both the experience we have been given in the life of Jesus and also in the radical message it sends out to us today.

God's Message for Today: Personal Transformation

First of all we have been given a clear vision of the *character* and *nature* of God, an image which had changed and grown throughout history until more deeply revealed in the life and teaching of Jesus. That revelation, we believe, has been given to us through the actual life and teaching of Jesus, revealing the true nature of the God in whom we believe, a God of compassion and love for each one of us.

This is not the God of retribution for the sins we all commit, whether in our own individual lives or in the world around us. It is the God of total love and compassion, a God of forgiveness, a God of healing (which is what the word *salvation* means) We are invited to turn our lives around so that we may be transformed and made *at one* with the loving God we see demonstrated in the life of Jesus. We see this in the traditional writings of the Orthodox Church. This is well portrayed in a book by John Meyendorff,[1] a notable Orthodox scholar of today, who observes that "the (Orthodox) Church baptizes children, not to visit their non-existent sins but to give them a new and immediate life, sharing in the communion of the body of Christ, participating in divine life, sanctification through the energy of God which penetrates true humanity and restores it to its natural state ... rather than the justification or remaining of inherited guild."

I pause at this moment to emphasize just how different is this image of the nature of God from the all too often picture of God not as a caring father but rather as the judge and tyrant which has infected so much of Christian thinking over the centuries especially in the Churches of the West. It is important to note that Christians of the Orthodox Churches have not been so infected. Their image is rather of a God of total love and compassion, a god of healing (which is what the word *salvation* is all about), a God who invites us to be open so that we might be transformed and be *at one* with God. To sum up, at the heart of Jesus' message, he is inviting each of us to set out on a journey of opening ourselves up to God so that we may each experience his compassion and love and so be personally transformed and, as I say in a prayer that I say each morning that I may "come to know God more clearly, love God more dearly and follow God more nearly day by day."

The Kingdom of God

But it does not end there. The God as revealed by Jesus is also giving us a *vision,* a vision of a new society a world transformed. This is where so many of the actions and sayings of Jesus are to be seen as a challenging new way at looking at the world around us. Throughout his ministry, we see and listen to Jesus challenging the world and society of his own day. He attacked a world in which the rich lorded over the poor, in which the sick and the beggars were cast out of society, in which those who were *different* were treated with contempt. We read again and again of Jesus railing at the injustices of his time, the arrogance of the rich and powerful, the overwhelming pride of the Sadducees and Pharisees, and the ways in which the sick were ignored and the poor treated with contempt. Instead, Jesus gave his followers a vision of a different kind of world, a vision not only about the overriding love and compassion of God for each individual but of God's deep concern for justice for all, so that all should be able to share in his creation and enjoy life in all its fullness and in which all would be treated with the compassion and acceptance which God has for each of us.

This was powerfully emphasized in the writings of Gerd Theissen,[2] a German theologian back in the 60's. What he high-lighted was the evidence that Jesus was indeed deeply concerned not only with specific people, such as the sick and poor to whom he ministered, but with the social and *political* issues of his day. The picture he sees in the gospels is that of a man who was highly critical of society as a whole, a person whom we would certainly describe as a *radical* in our own day. He was exhibiting his deep concern not only for the poor and down-trodden but also for the kind of society he was living in. What Theissen is bringing to light is a deeper understanding of the role that Jesus played in the society of his day. He was clearly attacking social poverty and indicating how it not only destroyed people's lives but lead to suffering and violence. The study of his ministry reveals his concern for the poor, the downcast and those who suffered from the injustices and power of others. It is clear that he had little time for the religious leaders and lawyers of his time. He was forceful in targeting the rich and the powerful who lorded themselves over others. He was certainly not just the milksop as displayed in the Sunday school pictures of him sitting with little children and playing with the lambs. He was a strong leader who had little good to say about the powerful and wealthy elites who looked down on the poor with contempt. It is quite clear that Jesus was not only a spiritual and compassionate man or someone who healed the sick and afflicted but also someone who had a vision. His message was not only a spiritual one, an invitation for each one of us to open our individual lives to God, but also a vision of our human society in God's world. It was this that led him to attack poverty, the practices of the rich and powerful and the systems of the time. Judea was at this time a turbulent country, often ridden with violence and suffering. The Jews hated their occupiers, although the rich were happy to live under their wings. The religious leaders clung to their place in society and were often more interested in the religious laws than in listening to the voice of God. In addition the Roman elite and army clung together in order to retain their power. The reaction of the Jewish people was inevitably to join together against the Romans and the power elites of their time, which often led to violence on both sides. Some of them, like the religious Essenes, simply closed together in communities and focused on their spiritual lives and traditions.

This was the living backcloth to what was going on in Judea in the time of Jesus but just where did he figure? Was he simply a spiritual leader, a teacher who had little to say about the society and world he was living in but spent his ministry healing the sick and comforting the downcast? Of course no one would deny that these took up a great part of his time and formed a considerable part of his ministry and teaching. What Theissen has made clear, however, was that Jesus also played a significant part in the social and political scene in the world of his time. What Jesus was doing was not only healing the sick and showing God's love for the downcast and marginalized in society but also giving us a vision of a world as God would have it. Not only are we all invited to open ourselves to a vision of love and compassion of God for each one of us but, as a society, we are given an equally important vision of the daily world in which we live today. Jesus has left us with a vision, not only of God's love and compassion for each individual but also a vision of God's deep concern for justice in society, so that all may be able to share in his creation and enjoy life in all its fullness. All of this is expressed in what Jesus called the *Kingdom of God* as is triumphantly proclaim in Handel's Messiah when we join in singing that "The kingdom of this world shall become the kingdom of Our God."

Notes

1. John Mayendorf. *Bysantine Theology: Historical Trends and Doctrinal Themes* (New York: Fordham University Press, 1978).

2. Gerd Theissen. *Sociology of Early Palestinian Christianity* and *The Shadow of the Galilean* (Philadelphia: Fortress Press, 1978).

Further Reading

Armstrong, David, ed. *The Truth About Jesus.* Grand Rapids: Eerdmans, 1998.

Borg, Marcus J., and N. T. Wright. *The Meaning of Jesus: Two Visions.* San Francisco: Harper, 1999.

Ingham, Michael. *Mansions of the Spirit: The Gospel in a Multifaith World.* Toronto: Anglican Book Centre, 1997.

Jenkins, Philip. *The Next Christendom: The Rise of Global Christianity.* Oxford: Oxford University Press, 2002.

Leech, Kenneth. *Subversive Orthodoxy: Traditional Faith and Radical Commitment.* Toronto: Anglican Book Centre, 1992.

Leech, Kenneth. *The Sky is Red.* London: Darton, Longman and Todd Ltd., 1997.

Polkinghorne, John. *The Way the World is: The Christian Perspective of a Scientist.* Louisville: Westminster John Knox Press, 2007.

Richardson, Alan. *The Political Christ.* London: S.C.M., 1976.

Schnell, Jonathan. *The Fate of the Earth.* New York: Knopf, 1982.

Temple, William. *Christianity and Social Order.* New York: Seabury Press, 1976.

Theissen, Gerd. *Sociology of Early Palestinian Christianity.* Philadelphia: Fortress Press, 1978.

Theissen, Gerd. *The Shadow of the Galilean.* Philadelphia: Fortress Press, 1978.

Vermes, Geza. *The Religion of Jesus the Jew.* Minneapolis: Fortress Press, 1993.

Chapter 5
Experience: The Golden Thread

One of the most important words as we seek the heart of the Christian faith is the word *experience* and there is good reason. So often religion seems to be a vast tangle of theology; whether it is Buddhism, Islam, Christianity, or one of t the dozens of other faiths in the world. But the reality is that what lies at the heart of all religions is not the words but the experience. Words are the creation of human beings who have struggled to understand and make sense of the world we live in. What lies at the heart of all religions is not words or theology but the experience of what I call the *Something More*. This is especially true of the Christian faith and is shared by all Christian believers throughout the world. It was a series of experiences which led to the birth of Christianity and it remains so to the present day. We are Christians now because of a series of experiences 2000 years ago in a tiny part of the Roman Empire followed by continuing experiences which continue to the present day.

It is significant that Dawkins cites the importance of *experience* as the most powerful argument for the existence of God. He writes: "The argument of personal experience is the one that is the most convincing to those who claim to have had one." However, he sarcastically goes on to make a mockery of such idiotic experiences as the claim to have seen a "pink elephant" or those "individuals in asylums who think themselves to be Napoleon Bonaparte or Charlie Chaplin or that the entire world is conspiring against them!"[1] He revels in attacking such experiences as "those seventy thousand pilgrims at Fatima in 1917 who saw the sun tear itself from the heavens and come crashing down on the multitude." Such gross distortions of the word experience are, of course, laughable and they certainly do not compare with the very real ways in which men and women have continued to experience God in their lives and the world around them. It is my point that such genuine experiences which are historically recorded in the New Testament and have continued in the lives of Christians until the present day are indeed at the heart of the Christian faith and constitute the *golden thread* to this day.

It was so at the very beginning. It was the experience of Jesus' reappearance right after his death that was to convince his followers of the presence of the *Something More* in him and which continued to convince them of his divinity.

That experience continued in the lives of his disciples, a body of men and women who came to be called the *Body* of Christ or, more simply, the *Church*. These words symbolized the living presence of this *Something More* which was experienced in several ways. One of these was recorded in Acts 9.36 ff, which tells of a woman called Tabitha, who had just died and whose body was being prepared for burial. It recounts how Peter prayed for her revival with the result that she sat up and rose to her feet, fully healed. We also read of the occasion when St Paul had a powerful vision on his way to arrest and detain all Christians in an attempt, shared by both Jews and Romans, to stamp out this radical new movement. The story tells how Paul had a shattering experience of the risen Christ who told him to proceed to the city of Damascus, where he would be met by leaders of the new Christian community which had grown up in the city. Once there, he would discover what God wished him to do. The rest of Paul's life is history but it was this vision which started it all.

The Experience of God in the Life of the Growing Church

As the new Christian movement continued to spread beyond Palestine, its numbers increased and expanded throughout the Eastern Mediterranean, reaching into the heart of the Empire in the Imperial city of Rome. During its early years, it was energized and held together by the continuing presence of God, which they expressed in the words *Holy Spirit*, describing God's Presence amongst them. The word *Spirit* appears resoundingly throughout all the early Christian documents. So important was this experience that Paul devoted a significant part of his many letters in describing this new reality and its power. In one of his letters to the Christians of Corinth, he specifically sets out to define the *fruits* (or outward expression) of this *Spirit* of God. We find a string of words such as insight, wisdom, healing and, most dramatically, what he called *glossalelia* or *speaking in tongues*. What is important is the reality of these things which actually happened, how in all of these different ways we can now sense the experiences of the people in those early days of the church as they were healed, given guidance, insight and fresh understanding. In the same letter to the Corinthians, Paul was to share experiences which displayed the love and the compassion of God amongst the Christian communities. It is also recorded in an interesting comment on the lives of those early Christians, when it was commonly remarked just "how they loved one another." What it also does for us, over 2000 years later, is to give us an insight into the loving *presence* of God, experienced in the lives of those early Christians.

One of Dawkins' most powerful critics and who was a contemporary of his at Oxford was John Polkinghorne, who points to the importance of experience in our understanding of God's reality. He writes of the importance of the risen Christ in the years that followed the resurrection as the Christians continued to experience this *Something More* in their personal and corporate lives. He points out that the doctrine of the Trinity which arose "is a response to the phenomenon which they experienced rather than the mere ungrounded metaphysical speculation." He points out "that the actual concept of the Trinity (i.e. Father, Son and Holy Spirit) was a summary of experience rather than a puzzling piece of divine arithmetic!"[2] His conclusion is that "What is at issue between (himself) and nonbelievers is the existence of a religious dimension to life, an experience of the 'other'."

As the Church continued to expand, this experience of the disciples continued. It was to be seen in the lives of the faithful as they continued to open themselves not only to the reality of God but also to the gift of His *presence* in and amongst them. Some of these came to be called *Saints*, a word simply meaning *holy* or *whole* people, who had allowed the *Something More* into their personal lives. Some of the most fervent faithful came to be called monks, usually living together in communities where they could follow the *new way* more nearly. The vast number, though, were ordinary people who came to know and sense this *spirit* in their daily lives. Some of them gave up their lives to be executed rather than deny the new reality that had come to be at the very centre of their new faith.

Experiencing God in the Developing Life and Traditions of the Church

From the very early days, those growing Christians began to develop special *ways* so that they could together grow and sense God in their own spiritual lives. We might think of these ways as being *aids* or *channels* through which they could be led to sense and experience God, both singly and together. In a similar way, the *structure* of the Church was seen as providing it with a kind of *body* of which they could be a part and within which they could each come to know the love and healing power of God. Some of these *ways* came to be what we now call the sacraments of the Church, ways in which we can experience the reality of God in our own lives. They have remained in the Christian community ever since.

At their core was and remains the *Eucharist,* a word literally meaning *thanksgiving*. Other names for it are the *Lord's Supper*, the *Holy Communion*, the *Mass* or the *Breaking of the Bread*. The practice of the Eucharist goes right back to the time just before Jesus' execution, when he shared the Last Supper with them and told them that when they shared a meal together in the future he would be with them. It left them with an indelible memory which they continued to honour each time they met together. Afterwards, this memory would remain as a powerful symbol of unity and mutual love, not only of them as a family of twelve but also as a growing family of all who were to follow in the *way* of Jesus. For the early Christian communities, the meal was experienced as the presence of God in their midst, a sign of their communion and of the mutual love which they shared. Paul was later to refer to these Eucharist's as "love feasts." At its heart, the Eucharist has continued to unite all Christians throughout the world as a joyful celebration of the reality and presence of the spirit of God within and amongst them. It is a *mystical* or numinous experience which, through time, has opened a channel through which we can sense and open our very being to the reality of God in our lives.

Another of these sacraments is called *Baptism* which is thought of by far too many people today simple as a ritual that a priest performs on a new born child largely as a symbol of its entry into the human world. Many years ago in Britain, a Cockney father once said to me, when I asked him why he wanted me to baptize his newly born child.

"Well," he said, "because he's British, like we are!" I burst out laughing. It was such a splendid response! But it did open my eyes to what so many people mistakenly believed about this so important sacrament. Baptism is not just *being British* or indeed or any other breed on earth! Rather it marks the beginning of the Christian journey in a person's life. It is the moment when a person opens him or herself to the God revealed by Jesus and begins to follow the *way* of God. In the case of an infant it is when the parents promise to bring him or her up as a Christian and the child is received into the family of the Church. Baptism is what happens when a person *turns* him or herself towards God with the intention of following and experiencing God for the rest of his life. If the child is part of a practicing Christian family, then it follows that baptism will most certainly make sense, so that he or she may continue to grow up in the faith if its parents. Baptism marks the spot when the person opens his heart in order to experience the reality of God in his own life.

The sacrament of *Confirmation* was later developed in the Church as a way of its members entering more deeply into the life of the church and so experiencing God as they continued to grow up. Both of these provide occasions within the Church's life when the whole community may not only welcome new *members* to its *body* but also give them selves opportunities of reopening themselves to the presence of the living God.

I will add one more Sacrament to the list. Like the others, it serves as a *way* or opportunity of being renewed during a Christian life. Its proper title is that of *Absolution,* when the emphasis upon what God is doing, rather than the person who has come to ask for it. It provides for an opportunity for those who have drifted away from God to turn around and open themselves to God's total forgiveness and grace. Again it is another opportunity to experience not only the reality but also the nature of the *Something More*. It is no coincidence that my wife clearly remembers the occasion when she was at a silent retreat led by an Anglican monk, together with a dozen or so members of my parish. At the end of the retreat, she made what was her first confession and a while later, after the priest pronounced her *absolution*, she experienced an overwhelming sense of the presence of God which had a profound effect on her and is remembered as a critical point in her spiritual life.

In the last few pages, I have tried to show how the theme of *experience* has resonated throughout the long story of the Christian Church and I have chosen to focus on some of the sacraments which are all about experiencing God, right from the cradle to the grave, opening windows through which we can *see* with our inner eyes the reality of the Something More so that, as I say in my prayers every morning, we may "follow God more nearly, know God more clearly and follow God more dearly, day by day."

This experience of God continues in the lives of people to this day who sense it in their very heart of their faith. Tom Harpur, a former columnist of the Toronto Star, Rhodes scholar and professor of Greek and the New Testament, expresses his own personal conviction of his own faith, as he writes: "I do experience God in a very personal way through his presence in my life and in the lives of those around me" and he goes on to add "we have an intuition down inside that knowing that transcendence even more fully, will transform our lives, not only once but as Paul says, 'from glory to glory'."[3] It was this powerful experience which empowered the lives of the early Christians, who went on to develop the their understanding of the Divine in the images of the Father, Son and Holy Spirit, i.e. the reality of God experienced in the Church and within themselves.

Experiencing God in My Own Personal Life

Like most Anglican children, I was confirmed in the Church when I was about thirteen years old and I have a clear memory of the occasion and of my sense of the Something More which I experienced. During the years that followed, the regular Eucharist increasingly deepened my sense of the *numinous*, the awareness of there being more to life than our material bodies. In the years that went by, I learned to see a quality of life in people of faith, a reality and quality which impressed me. This was enhanced in my later teens at boarding school, when I encountered a young Franciscan Friar for whom God was very real. From the regular worship in the school chapel, I often became aware of a sense of God's nearness. I deeply sensed *God* when I made my first confession and I continued to sense God's presence in the regular Eucharist and the simple reception of the earthly, yet holy bread and wine at the communion. In such ways, the sacraments certainly did their job. Not only did they act as powerful *symbols* of God's alleged presence but they also evoked a deep sense *of that* Presence, which has continued all of my life.

All of this raises a final and critical question. Is this experience really *real*?

This is ultimately a decision that we all have to make for ourselves. Is all the evidence of the experiences of Christian believers in the past enough to convince us that there is more than *just* an experience (like the taste of a good wine or the thrill of a winter's gale) but the experience of a *reality* that we call God? Is this God dead? I am myself convinced that the answer to both of these is a resounding "No!" I really do believe that there is Something More as experienced by Christians for over 2000 years and the reason for this is that they have come to *know* this God, as a reality in their own personal lives as well as in the life of the Church. Like them I also believe it for a second reason. It is because I have experienced this God powerfully in my own life. It is not only something that happened two thousand years ago and in then lives of others who have lived during that period. The fact is that God is to be experienced today, especially by those who open themselves to his presence and it is for this reason that, in the following pages, I have included quite a few of such experiences in the lives of both myself and in the lives of others whom I have known. God is indeed alive and well!

Some Personal Experiences: The Healing of People

In what follows I will be describing some forms of healing or *whole making* which I have experienced in the lives of others. Most of them happened in my own presence and, in several others, others were also often involved. The first of them took place when I was a young curate in a North London parish. Amy was a middle aged mother whose son went to the local school. On one of my early visits, I learned that she was suffering from the mental disease of agoraphobia, a terror of being outside. As a result she was confined to her home and it was there that I visited her regularly and realized just how extreme her confinement was. Shortly before I left the parish, I spent some time with her, praying with her that she might be healed of her sickness. I must admit that, at this point in my ministry, I had little expectation that my prayers would be of much help. After my departure, I continued to pray for her. Then, several months later, I received a letter from her together with a copy of the local newspaper. I was amazed when read the front page headline. It was all about Amy and how she had walked the High Street and herself collected over 2000 signatures in an attempt to get the local council to install a pedestrian crossing in that very busy part of the town. I soon learned that her agoraphobia had been totally healed soon after I had left the parish. My prayer had been answered.

Some years later I had come to be much more aware of the reality of experiences such as this. I was at this point rector of a parish in Montreal at a time when a movement of spiritual renewal was growing within the Christian church and at a time when the reality of God's presence was having a profound influence on many in the churches. As a consequence of this, the parish had invited Fr John Gunstone, a well known Anglican priest and author from England, to come and lead the parish in a week of spiritual renewal. Just before his arrival at the airport, we learned that a dynamic member of our parish team had been rushed to Montreal general hospital. Having been examined by the surgeon the day before the mission was to begin; the man was diagnosed with a dangerous blockage in his main artery and scheduled for an operation the following day. That same afternoon, we met John at the airport and related to him the bad news about the crisis. His response was to smile and say, "Then let's drive straight to the hospital, we need to have him with us tomorrow." We did so and went immediately to the ward. John introduced himself, listened to the story and then laid his hands on his body and prayed for the healing of his artery. Next morning we went again to the hospital and waited for the surgeon do his surgery. Before performing the surgery the surgeon performed tests to locate the exact position of the blockage. When he came to meet us in the hospital room he looked perplexed and said; "I can find nothing wrong with him. His artery is that of a young man!" It was a great start for all that followed. Another story tells of a World War 1 veteran called Jim. He was an office manager and also a key member of our Parish Council. He had a somewhat *crusty* personality and one who could be a strong negative influence, especially when it came to initiatives in the parish. He also had a difficult time dealing with old people and illness. However, somewhat to my surprise, I found him amongst a group of parishioners who were taking part in a series of discussions on spiritual growth. At the end of the course, I found myself laying my hands on Jim and, when I had finished, he raised his head and looked up at me. His face had a broad smile and there were tears rolling down his cheeks. Not only I but all those near him were amazed and, over the weeks that followed, many of them sought me out, remarking on the amazing transformation that had taken place in his personality. He rapidly became the most enthusiastic supporter and leader of some changes that were taking place in the parish and diocese and carried a smile every time that I saw him. Then, some months later, I had a call from the Bishop to say that Jim had approached him about his being ordained as a priest. Over the years that followed, he exercised a wonderful ministry in a local city parish and his special ministry was working with old people and those in hospital.

Healing in the Parish

There are many other stories which I would like to recount but there is just one which amazed both me and my wife. I am sure that, as you read it, you will agree that there is no possible explanation for it other than the sign which I will describe. It happened some years ago when I was rector of a large inner city parish. Things were not going well in the parish, so much so that I had come to the conclusion that I should consider resigning my position. I was in despair about my own ability to cope with the challenges and, one morning, I got to my knees and prayed to God for guidance and strength. I needed God's help and I needed it badly. Then a day or two later, I came home from work to be met by Sylvia telling me how, in her prayer time that morning, she had opened up her Jerusalem bible at random and said to God, very simply:

"Lord I know that we are not supposed to ask for signs but we need a sign right now." Then she looked down at the place where her finger was pointing and read some astonishing words which are worth quoting in full:

> This shall be the sign for you: thus shall be eaten the self-sown grain. Next year what sprouts in the fallow, but in the third year sow and reap. The surviving remnant of the House of Judah shall bring forth new roots below and above. For the remnant shall go out from Jerusalem and survivors from Mount Zion. The love of Yahweh Sabbaoth will accomplish this! (Isaiah 37.30-32)

The words hit her like a bomb and she was literally shaking when I got home. It was not difficult to decode the message. But there was more to come. The next morning, a student assistant of mine who was preparing for ordination called me from the college early in the morning and said: "Father Ian, I am not sure just why I am calling you but I would be grateful if I could see later this morning." I agreed and he duly came along shortly before lunch looking somewhat embarrassed. But what he had to say was both bizarre and mindboggling: "Father Ian, I was at my prayer time this morning when something prompted me to open up my bible. I did so and opened it at random. I read it but couldn't make any sense of it but something inside me said that I should call you and tell you about it, so here I am." It was, of course, the very same verses that Sylvia had read out to me the afternoon before. I am still in awe even as I write about it now. Needless to say, we did not leave the parish and it came as no surprise that the words proved themselves to be prophetic. The next couple of years were, indeed, tough but what came out of them was not only a fruitful ministry for me but also the resolution of a crisis with which the parish was wrestling. I will not go into details but will simply say that God breathed new life and resolve into the parish community and gave new life to my own ministry which had reached an all time low. It also demonstrated for me the reality of God and that he can sometimes answer a heartfelt prayer in the most unlikely ways!

I have included several other dramatic examples of people's experiencing of God in the section of this book called Something More. Of particular interest is Marcus Borg's book *Jesus* which focuses on the experiences of the early disciples, especially in the days after the execution of Jesus.

Notes

1. Richard Dawkins, *The God Delusion* (Boston: Houghtin Mifflin Co., 2006), 91-92.

2. John Polkinghorne, *The Way the World is: The Christian Perspective of a Scientist* (Louisville: Westminster John Knox Press, 2007), 98.

3. Tom Harpur, *Water into Wine* (Toronto: Thomas Allen Publishers, 2007), 222.

Chapter 6
Personal Transformation—The Problem: Human Sin

To this point, I have endevoured to present a case that God is real, that God *exists* and that we can experience God in our own physical lives. I have also attempted to describe just what this God is like, that he is not indeed the Old Testament God of fire and brimstone but the reality whom Jesus revealed as loving and compassionate. I have suggested that God invites us to open ourselves so that we can experience, not only the reality but the compassion that God has for us in our own individual lives. I have also suggested that God is inviting us to open ourselves and is calling us to set out on a journey, which I shall call a journey of transformation. However, there remains a stumbling block to embarking on the journey which was not only recognized by the Israelite people many centuries ago but also by every one of us today. It has been called human *sin*, a word with which we are familiar. What is it that lies at the root of this human urge that so distorts our lives? Someone tried to answer this question about 3,000 years ago by telling the story of Adam and Eve in the Garden of Eden. In writing it, the writer was trying to grasp the reality of human sin and how it came to be a reality in all our lives. The story may be out of date but the reality of sin is just as much a reality as it was in his own life and in the world in which he lived. If we are to embark on any kind of journey of personal transformation today, then we need to recognize the hard truth about this *flaw* in our own lives today. It is a flaw we each have within ourselves and it affects not only each one of us but also the world in which we live. If we are indeed to set out on this journey of transformation, then we need some meaningful *markers* to help us on our way. We need a 21st century model based upon what we know about both human personality and the nature of the God revealed to us in the person of Jesus. This I will endeavor to do in what now follows and I will also suggest practical ways in which each of us can set about our own personal spiritual journey. In the two sections which follow, I will suggest two images, the first of which is based on the insights of psychical studies and the second drawn from the Gospel of Luke (15.11-32). In the diagram that follows I have illustrated the journey in the course of which we are invited to open ourselves to the reality of God in our lives especially, as we share in the worship and sacraments of the Church with our fellow Christians.

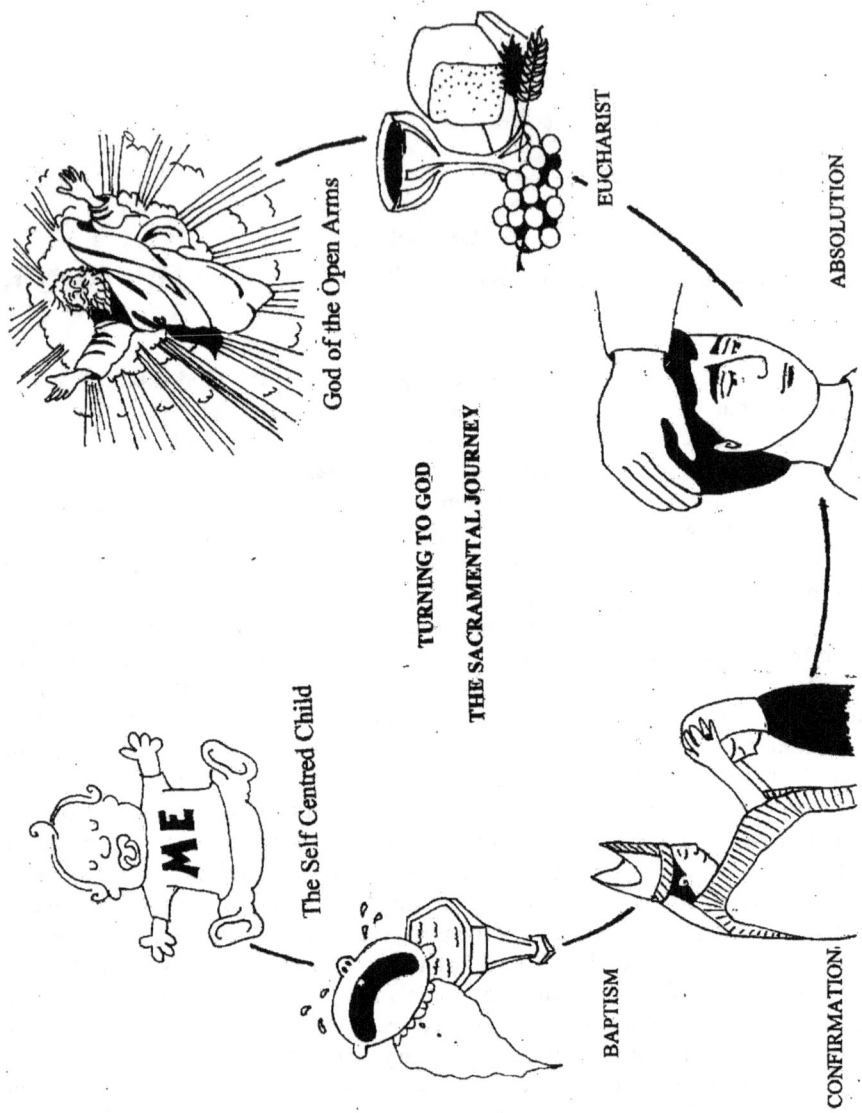

Chapter 6

The Image of the Self Centered Child

I will begin with the moment of our individual human birth, the moment when we come into the world as a tiny child. I am going to use an image which is drawn, not from the Bible but from the works of one of the fathers of psychology, Carl Jung. Since his time science has developed in many directions (largely to do with the physical functioning of the human brain and the use of chemicals) but his studies into human behaviour remain and provide us with a considerable insight into the ways we function in the world as individuals. In particular, Jung has left us with a powerful image of how each one of us experiences his or her individual *self* and of how that experience can come to dominate what drives us in life and the way we see and feel ourselves in relation to the wider world around us. What all this reveals is a built-in *egocentricity*—a picture of *me* at the centre and the rest of the outside world as serving only my own egocentric needs and feelings. It is what I call my egotistic *inner child*. This *inner child* is quite evident from the very moment of its birth. As parents we are thrilled with the joy of this moment and, as the weeks go by, we see the smile on the babies face, the way in which it recognizes its mother and the warmth in its eyes. However, there is also the not-so-nice baby, the baby who is very much the centre of its own life and world; the baby who demands immediate attention and screams when it doesn't get any. This inner drive continues from birth onwards. Few things are more powerful in the life of a growing child. In fact this reality is a part of its natural instinct for survival which later leads to both the destructive ways we behave in human groups leading to tribal warfare and to the self-centered politics of nations and institutions, but also to the creative drive we need to survive as human beings. I would like to suggest that it is the negative side of this reality which, in theological circles, is called *sin*, a powerful word that resounds in the Bible and the teachings of Jesus, as well as in other religions. It is how we are born and it is a driving force in each one of us. It is that egocentricity within us all from the moment of our birth. It is what I call the destructive *Inner Child*. The question that arises from this insight is very simple. Just how is it to be dealt with, how can the destructive *inner child* be reformed so that he or she and the whole of society be *healed*? I suggest that we have the answer in the second of the images which follows.

The Image of the God of the Open Arms (Luke 15.11-32)

One of the parables that Jesus told was of a wealthy landowner who had two sons. The younger one, having become tired of living on the family estate, decided to claim his inheritance and launch out into the wider world. So he went off, taking his money with him and set about enjoying the high life of the big city. The story tells of how he flung himself into its life of booze, gambling and all its pleasures. Inevitably, he lost all that he had and turned his back on the city and began to set out for home, bitterly regretful and dressed in rags. He reached home and prepared himself to face his angry father. But now the focus changes from the son to the father, a father whom the son feared would turn his back and close the door to him. But an amazing thing happened. As the son drew near, he saw that his father had opened the gate and was running to greet and embrace him. The father's face was full of tears and joy. He hugged his son, called for a great feast to celebrate his return and offered him a generous share of the estate, an act which went against the Jewish laws of the day and no doubt shocked his neighbours.

This story, more than any other image of God in the Bible, most deeply and powerfully illuminates the true *nature* of God. It was very different from the Jewish concept of God of the time. It displays what I call the *God of the Open Arms*, the God who is a God of infinite compassion and acceptance, a God whose arms are always open to receive us when we return, ready to accept God's reality and love, a God who accepts us for who we are. God is not one who judges us by our behaviour when we recognize our failures and turn ourselves around.

What It Is All About?

These two examples, one of the God of the open arms and the other of the egocentric nature of each one of us, have helped me to get a practical image of what our own individual journey in this world is all about. It is in fact a journey of transformation, a radical transformation from being a totally egocentric person to one whose whole being is opened to the reality of the *God of the Open Arms*. It is a journey that begins with a turning towards God, committing ourselves in faith, sensing God's presence and action in our own lives, allowing God to *heal* and enlighten us so that we can come to understand the reality of things as God sees them, allowing ourselves to be forgiven from all the negative things in our lives so that we may enjoy life in all its fullness and come to know God's presence day by day. Now that's quite a vision but it is no more than Jesus was revealing and offering to us. We call it a journey of transformation.

Transformation in the Body of Christ

To this point I have focused on our own personal journeys but there is more. We are not alone but are members of the Church, which St Paul described as the Body of Christ. We are not left to ourselves on the journey. Within the *body* we are given opportunities of experiencing the presence of God not only in the Christian fellowship but in what are called the sacraments of the church which give us opportunities to come to know God in our daily lives. This I have tried to point out in a diagram which illustrates the *journey* we share as members of the body of Christ.

Personal Transformation and Spiritual Growth

It is significant that, for many searching people, the word *spirituality* is now becoming almost a buzz word. While I am somewhat glad about its higher profile, I am also somewhat concerned about what people really think it means. To some it indicates simply a widespread feeling that there must surely be some kind of *reality* other than the physical or, maybe, that there is some kind of phenomenon which science will one day be able to explain and define, in other words that the *Something More* is no more than a nice feeling. However as I have made very clear, I believe that there is indeed something more whom we call God and that, as we open our lives we will sense the reality of God. Spirituality, in fact, is all about coming to know and experience this reality in our personal lives, to come to "know God more really, to follow God more nearly and to love God more dearly, day by day," as an old prayer puts it. Marcus Borg reminds us of this when he writes: "The Christian life is not very much about believing a set of beliefs, but about a deepening relationship with the one in whom we live and move and have our being."[1] More and more people of faith are learning that spiritual growth has indeed been a traditional and continuing practice in the Church. However it is often ignored in the lives of many who call themselves Christians. I am reminded of an elderly woman who came regularly to church, when discussing the topic of spiritual growth she said that "she never thought about such things"! Yet spirituality should be the very life line of our journey as followers of Christ in our daily life. It is indeed sad that so much of what we think of as *religion* has to do almost exclusively with finances, parish meetings, buildings, forms of service, social activities, administration etc but preciously little to do with any kind of individual spiritual growth. We need to remind ourselves that the spiritual journey is not just for saints, monks and clergy persons or spiritually *holy* people. Spirituality and spiritual growth is for all Christians. It is the lifeline of our faith and practice and part of our every day lives. The American thinker and politician Al Gore put it in this way when he said on television "Many have left organized religion and yet continue to harbour a continuing sense of the *Something More*. My point is that they have left an opportunity of developing their sense to grow and develop and transform their lives." Certainly, saying the Lord's Prayer is a good idea but the spiritual journey is about much more. Spiritual growth or getting to know the God of the Open Arms better is basically simple but it does require time and commitment. One critically important aide in achieving this is to have the support and guidance from someone who is able to guide and encourage us on our personal journey. Sometimes it is as simple as having a wife or husband who shares their faith just as they share our ordinary daily lives. But it is also of great help if we have someone who is, maybe, a few steps ahead of us in our faith journey, someone who by their own experience and training can help us along the *way*. We talk of this as *Spiritual Direction*. It is meant to be one of the skills of the parish priest but not all of them posses that particular gift. That is not a negative observation but simply a truth and we do not always find this gift in our own local clergy person, gifted though they he or she may be in other matters. So we need to search out to find someone else who might be a spiritual companion to help us along our own unique journey. Such companions do not necessarily have to be ordained and we can usually find a compatible person if we take the trouble to seek them out. Sometimes spiritual companions or directors are to be found in various religious houses if there is one conveniently located. Sometimes our parish priest will recommend someone, male or female, who has this gift and maybe, training. In one town I lived in there was a very effective Catholic Order that specialized in this and they were very much kept busy by providing not only regular spiritual direction for individuals but opportunities to share regular periods of silence at the Centre every week. Some years ago in the another Diocese in which we were living, I observed many for whom the need for such spiritual direction was so pressing that we had to train a significant number of spiritual directors to meet the demands of the parishes. As a result, a growing number of people learned the value of their own spiritual growth, of how to pray, to meditate, to go on retreats, to follow the *Lectio Divina*, to fast, to tithe and contribute towards motivating the congregation as a whole to move forward. It is up to each of us to reach out, to share our journeys with others and to seek guidance wherever we can find it.

Spiritual Growth of the Church Community

In all of these ways above, it is clear that our own spiritual growth can be achieved by a significant number of ways but I would like to add another which is traditional and basic. I am talking about the whole Christian community which welcomed us into its body when we were baptized and which continues to feed and nourish us as we grow as its members, all of us sharing in our common experience of the risen Christ and the *real* presence of the Spirit of God in our midst. This presence of the Spirit in a local church reveals itself in the character of the community. This was how it was in the very beginning of the Church and it continues to be a mark of a parish which has truly allowed itself to be open and strong in its faith. I know that many of the congregations I have come to know have all experienced this presence. St Paul commented on this characteristic, long ago, when he observed that local people had been heard to remark "How those Christians love one another." One of the reasons that the first Christians met together was that they could all support and share their experience of God with each other. It was this simple fact that gave the early Christians the faith to face the attacks of their opponents and even arrest and death. There is no questioning that they were very much aware of the presence of God in their own lives and in the life of the Church of which they were a part. This is not true of a significant number of congregations today where the sense of God's presence may sometimes be sadly lacking. I have experienced occasions when I have gone to a Sunday morning service and have looked about for someone who might smile but all I saw and continued to see were people's backs. Hardly anyone spoke to me and the message was clear. One of the joys of the parish, in which we are now living in our retirement, has been to see the immediate warmth that greeted us on our very first visit. This, we immediately decided, was where we belonged.

It is also sad to often not experience any sense of the spiritual in the Sunday worship, a sense of the presence of God in the music and images of the liturgy, in the singing of the hymns, in the palpable silences, in the people coming to receive healing in some quiet part of the church and, above all, in the sense of God's presence on the faces of those around us.

The lack of such experiences is often displayed by the frequent lack of any mention of anything remotely *spiritual* in the affairs and communications of the same parishes. So many congregations spend long hours discussing finances, how to attract people to come to church, organize parish suppers, deal with the rain coming through the roof, but whose members rarely meet to discuss their spiritual journeys both individually or as a Christian family.. This became very clear to me one day in a meeting of my parish committee, where, as in most of our parishes, it was so easy to leave God out of the agenda. This had certainly been the case in many of our meetings but one day it changed. Shortly before this, I encouraged all the members of the Committee to spend a weekend at a *renewal* conference that was taking place in the city. A week later, instead of focusing on the usual matters of finance and buildings, the most unlikely person spoke up and moved a motion that every week the committee should meet for a simple meal and a chance to pray together, as well as the usual monthly committee meeting. It was passed by everyone. The difference in the committee meetings that followed was experienced by all. The presence of God had become *real* and palpable. The point I am making here is that spiritual growth is not only for each individual but for the Christian community as a whole. For this reason, I am convinced that every opportunity must be given, especially to those who are the leaders and *doers* in the church, committee members, wardens, treasurers and leaders of all kinds, to go on group retreats, be involved in education programmes, share in regular corporate prayer with others, seek spiritual directors, use the parish library and take every opportunity to grow in their experience of the love and vision of God.

We all need to allow ourselves and our local church to be open to the *holy*, which is what our faith and traditions are all about. When it comes down to it, worship is all about experiencing the numinous, the *holy* the *Something More* whom we call God, amongst us and in all that we are doing. This is why we need to pay so much attention to the ways we come together with our fellow Christians especially when we join each other for our weekly celebration of the Holy Communion or Eucharist.

Just what is it that leads many Christians to simply stop going to church and especially to the Holy Eucharist? I suggest that we need to ask just what it was that brought so many people who went in the past. Was it simply because it was the thing to do on Sunday mornings? Was it the smell of incense, the sound of music, the Rector's sermons or, maybe, to meet our friends? Was it also that *churchgoing* had become part of a culture that has slowly died out? For many younger people especially today this *culture* is a thing of the past in a rapidly changing world. Why shouldn't we stay in bed on Sundays, sit in front of the computer or go to play with our friends? Is the Eucharist just a thing of the past? Just what is so unique about this tradition which has lasted for over 2000 years, a tradition which has been at the heart of the Christian faith and practice?

To respond to this, we need to go back to the historical moment when a man called Jesus gathered together a small group of followers whom he called his disciples. They shared his presence when he was alive with them leading up to the night of his arrest. On that night he broke bread and drank wine with them and instructed them to continue to do this, whenever they met together, to recall his presence. Then immediately after his crucifixion, they continued to meet together to eat and drink and in doing so they experienced his presence amongst them and in their own personal lives. In the years that went by, his followers continued to come together to share bread and wine and in doing so continued to experienced the presence of God both in their communities and in their individual lives just as the disciples had done in the past. This meal has become and remains at the heart of the Christian faith and practice. It is a celebration of the presence and experience of a *Something More* both individually and in the *body* of the Christian community. The Eucharist is all about the coming together of the Christian community, sometimes called the *body of Christ*, a gathering of Christian people who share the experience of the *Something More* in their both in our own individual lives and also in the gathering which they called the *church* just as it was 2000 years ago.

So I suggest that we ask ourselves some important questions. Do we open ourselves and our fellow Christians to sense the spirit of God in the music that we join in singing? Does it raise our spirits to the presence of God amongst and within us? Does it express the presence of the divine healer in our midst and do we really expect him to heal us? One of the gifts of the renewal movement was that it brought so many local churches literally to their *senses* as they sensed the presence of God amongst their communities. Do we see sheer joy when we look around us? Does the *peace* really express the unity and love for each? Is it not this that inspires us to be in Church as we share in the experience of the *Holy* amongst our fellow Christians Sunday by Sunday? If not, why not? Maybe many of us need to get together to ask ourselves some of these questions and maybe open our eyes and our hearts to the reality of the God who is in our midst. I hope that this leaves us on a high rather than a sigh. For many of us this experience of the presence of God in our Christian community is a wonderful reality, for others perhaps a vision of what could be. It is certainly a vision of God, a vision which lies at the heart of our faith and our own personal journey as we open ourselves to experience the reality of the presence of the loving and compassionate God. It is a vision which we can realize as we come to know and be made *whole* as we day by day allow God into our hearts and minds.

Notes

1. Marcus J. Borg, *The Heart of Christianity: Rediscovering a Life of Faith* (San Francisco: Harper, 2003) p.120

Further Reading

Many of the books which follow were written during the latter part of the 20th century when there was a revival of spiritually which had a profound effect on many people within the churches. Many of these books are highly relevant in today's world and are certainly available through major distributors via the internet. For this reason, I am including them in the list that follows. Such books would be especially valuable if shared with a spiritual advisor.

Borg, Marcus J., and N. T. Wright. *The Meaning of Jesus: Two Visions*. San Francisco: Harper, 1999.

Cullman, Oscar. *The State in the New Testament*. London: S.C.M., 1957.

Gore, Al. *Earth in the Balance: Ecology and the Human Spirit*. Emmaus, PA: Roledale Press, 2006.

Ingham, Michael. *Mansions of the Spirit: The Gospel in a Multifaith World*. Toronto: Anglican Book Centre, 1997.

Jenkins, Philip. *The Next Christendom: The Rise of Global Christianity*. Oxford: Oxford University Press, 2002.

Leech, Kenneth. *Subversive Orthodoxy: Traditional Faith and Radical Commitment.* Toronto: Anglican Book Centre, 1992.

Leech, Kenneth. *The Sky is Red.* London: Darton, Longman and Todd Ltd., 1997.

Mayendorf, John. *Bysantine Theology: Historical Trends and Doctrinal Themes.* New York: Fordham University Press, 1978.

Polkinghorne, John. *The Way the World is: The Christian Perspective of a Scientist.* Louisville: Westminster John Knox Press, 2007.

Richardson, Alan. *The Political Christ.* London: S.C.M., 1976.

Schnell, Jonathan. *The Fate of the Earth.* New York: Knopf, 1982.

Temple, William. *Christianity and Social Order.* New York: Seabury Press, 1976.

Theissen, Gerd. *Sociology of Early Palestinian Christianity.* Philadelphia: Fortress Press, 1978.

Theissen, Gerd. *The Shadow of the Galilean.* Philadelphia: Fortress Press, 1978.

Vermes, Geza. *The Religion of Jesus the Jew.* Minneapolis: Fortress Press, 1993.

Chapter 7
The Kingdom of God:
The Vision of a
Transformed World

In the last chapter, we were invited to open ourselves and to grow and experience God through our own personal lives. I call this the Christian way or journey as I have already indicated, the way we can each come to know and experience God in our daily lives. This is what our regular prayers, the sacraments and the living reality of the Holy Spirit in the daily life in the Body of Christ is all about. As we have seen, all of this is at the heart of our personal journey.

But now I turn to the second vision which Jesus left to us, a vision of how we might live in this down-to-earth world of which we are all a part. It is part of a vision of a totally transformed world, a world as God would have it, the physical and the social world in which we all live. Jesus referred to it as the *Kingdom of God* and it is of this vision that I would now be focusing in the final section of the book. But, first of all, let us take a look at the world in which we are all living in today.

Today's World

I will begin with where we are now with a world which confronts us every day of the week. The world of shopping and bringing up families, the world of finance and business, the world of science and technology, the world of war and hunger, the world of our everyday lives. I read the national and the local newspapers almost every day, I religiously turn on the late night News before going to bed and often browse the TV channels which certainly exhibit that world in all its glory and weaknesses. And what a world it is! Sometimes I am uplifted and warmed by what I see, often it leaves a broad grin on the faces of my wife and me and occasionally I am inspired by this world, especially the bits of it I like. But, far too often, after I have watched the National on the CBC, I go to bed sad and even angry.

I am so aware of the frightening shadow side of the world. It is a world of vast, almost unimaginable wealth alongside the most abject poverty. Some time ago, I watched a movie of the enormous riches that were displayed in the Gulf City of Dubai, a city set in a part of the world torn by poverty and violence. *(Note: Even as I am reading this somewhat later to myself, it is ironic to listen to the radio and hear that the city is now in a situation of economic collapse.)* We live in an economically global and unstable world where vast corporations exercise power and influence not only over individual nations but over governments and the economies of nations all over the world. It is a world of both huge wealth and vast areas of families living in acute poverty and sickness. As I write this now, the world is going through a period of economical collapse, leading to unemployment, increasing poverty and social unrest. War and terror seem to have us in their grip, with all their tragic consequences, while race and religion become tools of violence and hate. Is this the kind of world that God would wish? Is the main purpose of the spiritual life simply to provide comfort, reassurance and inspiration only in our own daily lives ... or is it to challenge, confront and transform the world we live in? This vision is certainly what the teaching of Jesus was all about and it was no doubt the reason he was done-away with. This vision is one of the most constant themes spread throughout the Bible and which is expressed constantly in the teachings of Jesus. The word justice is a word which continues to ring loudly and insistently throughout both the old and the new testaments. It under lays the message of the prophets, who constantly taught the way of *justness,* or that which was *right* (*tsedek* in the Hebrew) and it was at the centre of Jesus' teaching. It rings out in the Gospels and it lies at the centre of many of the parables. It was used in the individual sense of being honest and in being *just* the whole social scene in the world in which they lived. God is portrayed by Jesus as being passionately concerned, not only with people's individual lives but with the social order in which they lived, a vision of a new way of living, a vision Jesus expressed in the image of the *Kingdom of God*. Sadly, one of the unfortunate directions in the theology of the mediaeval times was to interpreted this vision as pointing to what happens to us after we die (that is, only after we have first behaved ourselves here on earth). But it is now quite clear that, although there was certainly an element of this in Jesus' teaching, the phrase *Kingdom of God* was rather a vision of what *might be* here on earth. There is no doubt that Jesus was concerned with each individual's person's sin, as I have indicated in the previous chapter. Jesus clearly displays God's deep love for each one of us and passionately wishes us to come to be transformed and come to know God more and more. However, he has also given us a vision of a new order here on this earth, a new way of thinking and living, a vision of a new world, the *Kingdom of God*. This has become quite clear in studies over the last century and has resulted in a broad field of thinking and action as we try to apply it to our world of today. As Stewart Headlam, a Christian author of the 20th century put it: "Not a single word was uttered by Jesus about life after the grave. Rather, his words tell of a Kingdom of Heaven to be set up on earth as a righteous society." What, then, does this vision have to say to us in today's deeply divided and frightened world? Surely Headlam is reminding us that, when Jesus spoke of the *Kingdom of God*, he was speaking, not of what happens to us after we die but giving us a new vision of the world, not only in his own time, but also in the down to earth world in which we live today and in the centuries to come. Jesus was giving his followers a vision of a righteous and just society, a new way of living on earth. Headlam points out that the concern of Jesus was all focused on people, not just as individuals but as a whole society. Harvey Cox, an influential writer of the sixties, also wrote a penetrating book called *The Secular City* in which he drew a picture of the influence of the then-growing *God is Dead* movement, especially in North America. His book illustrates many of the influences which were making their impact on the rapidly changing of then world at that time. While he radically throws out many of the traditional concepts of the church, he shows how the vision of the Kingdom of God in the teachings of Jesus provide us with a powerful new vision of the world we live in today. In his writings, he argues that: "The starting point for any theology of the church today must be a theology of social change." Following this, Alan Richardson, the Dean of York Minster in England also wrote a short volume called *The Political Christ* in which he points out the truly *political* contents of Jesus' teachings and their relevance in our world of today. Even before these writers, William Temple, Archbishop of Canterbury during and after the Second World War, displayed a clear vision of the relevance of the Kingdom of God to the situation of his own time and exercised considerable influence in the Parliament in England.

In Germany, the image of the Kingdom of God was inspired by a theologian called Martin Bonhoeffer (1906-45), whose life and writing had profound effect on the thinking that followed the same war. He was eventually executed by the Nazis for his opposition to all that had been going on in his country and, in the giving of his life, he was pointing out two things. Firstly, he made it clear that each of us must grow personally in our own lives as we allow ourselves to be transformed by God. He said that Jesus had given us a vision of the *Kingdom of God*, a vision of a new kind of world, a world as God would have it, a world based on justice and compassion. This self-giving love was expressed in his own personal life when he suffered execution by the Nazis. However, his thinking was to have a powerful effect during the years that followed. Some years later and in another part of the world, these images of the Kingdom of God were to have a powerful effect in South America, which at time was facing revolution and political turmoil. Great concern was expressed by a number of Catholic clergy as they tried to come to terms with what was going on in their countries. One of these was the Brazilian Rubem Alves (1933—). He argued that the idea of the word *love* in the gospels had become sentimentalized and made the excuse for inaction in the face of injustices. As a result, he called for action that would liberate people from their past history, a process which led to the so-called *Liberation Theology* and the practical effects that followed. Even though this was seen by many as being influenced by the communist writings of Karl Marx, it also expressed the influence of the image of the Kingdom of God which his own Catholic background proclaimed.

Another writer, Gustavo of Peru, was also inspired by this image of Jesus, which led to his becoming involved in the revolutionary politics of his time. Although some regarded this as support of armed protest, it succeeded in inspiring a new sense of freedom to the underprivileged of Latin America, a freedom which, at best, gave them a new sense of their values and a spirit of cooperation in building a *new world* in their own society. The movement was embraced especially amongst the poorer people in their efforts to escape from the historical domination of the old Spanish classes and was centered on building up a more just society. As a result of what was going on in Southern America, it is significant that this vision was publicly endorsed and encouraged by Pope Paul in a 1979 speech in Rome, in which he spoke of the *bringing together* of liberation and the gospel, insisting on the church's duty to speak out on behalf of all victims of injustice. During his message, the Pope said: "So liberation is certainly a reality of faith, one of the biblical themes which are part of Christ's saving mission of the work of redemption and of his teaching." The vision of the Kingdom of God, here in our own world, is indeed at the heart of the Christian faith.

Liberation in Practice

I myself had a small insight of what liberation meant to the villagers of a small village in the Mexican countryside some years ago. I still have a clear memory of spending some time talking with a group of Christians. There were many such small groups in that place and in the surrounding country side, often supported by their priests who saw, in what was going on, the hand of God in truly *liberating* the poor and powerless. It was a thrilling experience and in such groups I was impressed with the total absence of violence and how amazing things happened—like the raising of a new school building almost overnight, a task they had been forbidden to undertake. But I was even more impressed with the genuinely Christian motivation and enthusiasm of those people and the brave leadership of many of their clergy and leaders in an attempt to *build the kingdom* in the form of a local school which would give new hope and opportunity for the growing children of their community. During that time, I met and talked with a number of poor people who would get together, usually with their local priest, to set about transforming their communities, often against the opposition of the police and landlords. At the heart of these, often illegal, activities were the Christian groups that met regularly for prayer leading into action and, often, persecution. They were a reminder of the vision of the coming of the *Kingdom of God* in those communities.

I will conclude with a few more vignettes in which I had the experience of meeting personally with some amazing men and women who had not only come to know God in their lives but also to exhibit God's presence in their willingness to bring about the Kingdom of God in society, even to the extent of offering their own lives.

Chapter 7

I have a vivid memory of Father Trevor Huddleston in Cambridge, just after he had been compelled to leave South Africa by the apartheid government there. He was an Anglican monk who had been very much involved in supporting the black Africans in their struggles with the government, risking his life many times and being regarded as something of a saint. He had just returned to England after having faced up to the guns and tanks of the Apartheid government as they lay waste the houses and fired ruthlessly upon the backs of the black people. His name had become legend in England and, even though only at just a few hours notice, he packed the large building in Cambridge with students like myself. He was a gaunt, passionate man who had given his life to God and lived it out against the cruel regime in the South Africa of the time. He was indeed a man of God with a profound understanding of what it meant to "seek first the Kingdom of God."

Some years later, during the years when I was at the Cathedral in Montreal, I was instrumental in arranging a special luncheon in honour of another *saint* of our time. His name was Helda Camerra, the Archbishop of Recife in Brazil who happened to be in Montreal at the time. He was a visionary who shared the ideas of the liberal activists of the time and who championed the rights of the poor in Latin America. He was especially concerned about the workers in a very large and powerful Canadian Company which had its head office in Montreal. A friend of mine was a colleague of the company president whom he persuaded to arrange and preside at a lunch, to which I was invited. I shall never forget the atmosphere of the lunch as the company president listened to what Helda Cammara had to say, as he spoke of the people and the poor conditions of his country Brazil and was quite open in addressing himself to many of the poor working conditions in the president's own company. It was an amazing coming together of truth and love. At one point I sat and watched the tears on the president's face. Sadly, no miracles occurred but the subject had been exposed. Helda Camarra returned to his own country where he daily went in danger of his life. It was a powerful experience to be with a man of God and I will never forget it. Sometime later, I found myself in the Cathedral of Cuernavaca in Mexico for the Sunday Mass. It proved to be a remarkable occasion. It was a colourful and enthusiastic High Mass, presided over by the Bishop and attended by a huge crowd of people from far and wide, marking the anniversary of the assassination of Archbishop Oscar Romero, a man of God who had given his life for the poor of his country. It was another experience of a man who had taken the message of the *Kingdom* to heart and showed his faith by giving up his life. Such another man was Martin Luther King of America, who equally shared the vision of the Kingdom of God.

These are some of the outstanding people whom I have experienced in my own life, men and women who have been prepared to give their lives as a result of their vision. I have also experienced others nearer to home who have personified the centrality of that vision in their lives and activities. One was Ted Scott, Primate of the Anglican Church of Canada in the seventies and eighties, whose ministry was very much bound up with the bringing about of the *Kingdom* in Canada and abroad. I had the privilege of getting to know him well and witnessing his passion for the poor and the aboriginal peoples of the country, a vision that spread throughout the world in his presidency of the World Council of Churches and, especially, in the work of the Primate's World Relief and Development Fund.

The Kingdom of God in My Own Ministry

Right at the start of my ministry as a parish priest, the Kingdom of God has always played a significant part. In my very first job as a curate in London, I recollect going public in revealing the tactics of some landlords in the parish, who were using all kinds of abusive and illegal tactics in making money out of poor tenants. It was picked up by the press and I nearly ended up, on the local council. Thankfully, I soon left that parish for one of my own. Years later, at the Anglican cathedral in Montreal, I remember leading the Sunday congregation down to the subway station after the Eucharist, with banners urging the authorities to allow cheaper fares for senior citizens. On another occasion, I took part in a *sit in* at one of the city's Social Security offices, protesting the low rates of the city's social support system. Thankfully, I was not arrested. Those were the days! I also moved a motion regarding a Guaranteed Annual Income at our Diocesan Synod. This passed with a comfortable margin but was ignored by the Federal Government. What I am trying to express is how the message of Jesus applies not only to our individual transformation and growth but also upon our willingness to dedicate ourselves to the fulfillment of the vision of God for the world in which we live.

I will conclude with a story about a very special lady whom I will never forget, a woman who was very close to God even up to the point of giving up her own life. She was the president of the Black YWCA in South Africa and had been the guest of the Anglican Church in Canada and was to return home by air that afternoon. During lunch at our Rectory, she told us what it was like being black in the segregated country and she expressed her fear of returning there, where she would probably face arrest and imprisonment because of the things she had been speaking about while in Canada. She was a woman of deep faith and wanted nothing but peace and justice in her own country. She had a profound affect on our own family. After lunch, we took her to the airport and made our farewells. Before she left, she said that she was in fear of what would happen to her on arrival in South Africa. That was the last anyone saw of her. She simply disappeared. Maybe she was killed. Nobody ever knew.

The Kingdom of God in Today's World

In the time which has elapsed over the last few decades, the challenges have become even greater. The wave of militant Islam has increased in the Middle East with the inevitable loss of human lives and the spread of violence in many parts of the globe. The recent collapse of the global economic markets is a result of human greed which has left large numbers of unemployed workers and the draining of national resources.

The effects of climate change are beginning to be felt and the world is beginning to wake up to radical changes which need to be made and accepted. Poverty and hunger continue to ravage vast numbers of people, especially in the less *developed* parts of the world. Weapons of mass destruction continue to be developed and armies continue to grow, whether they are tribal militias or huge forces, as in the United States. More than ever before in human history has the vision of the *Kingdom of God* been more relevant. I have endeavoured to show the centrality of the *Kingdom of God* in the teaching of many thinkers and activists over the latter part of the 20th century, which has revealed the critical importance of the *Kingdom of God* in the teachings of Jesus and what it has come to mean in how people live, both then and now. But just as we are led to these insights, so we are led to a challenging question: just what are the practical implications for today? Just how are we to approach bringing about this vision of God's world? Over the last few years, writers like Al Gore in America have been urging us to open our eyes to the enormous challenge of climate change and the ways in which we continue to ravage the environment. Madeline Albright has published a book challenging the new President of the United States to seek news ways in bringing about greater global peace and justice in the world. This leads us to the final question: What can we do to make a better world?

Human Poverty

Perhaps most obvious is the fact that a huge proportion of the human race are living in abject poverty and hunger, not only in the so-called *third world* but in the societies of those who are reading this book. Today we are faced with an ever growing number of those living in abject poverty with all its implications. This is nothing new but it is becoming a threat as never before. I have no need to cite the enormous challenge in extreme and growing poverty in today's world. It is staring us in the face both abroad and at home, even in the most advanced nations. It was said 25 years ago that, in 83% of the population in growing countries, only 3 percent of the people owned or controlled 80% of the agricultural land. These figures might be worse in the world of the 21st century when war, violence and climate change continue to deepen the pit of poverty into which so many people have fallen. While this continues to be catastrophic in much of the developing world, poverty is still endemic in our own *developed* societies where many still go hungry, many rely on handouts. Food banks and drop-in centers are unable to cope and a significant percentage of children are going to bed hungry and falling out of the education system. Poverty remains a continuing challenge in our own world just as it was in the days of Jesus. It is more than significant that Jesus himself showed a deep compassion for the poor and he was known and often opposed for this in the society of his own day. The cry of the poor throughout the world and the vision of a just society remain significant components in the vision of God as seen in Jesus.

The Social Order

It is abundantly clear that it is not only in our individual lives but also in the overall social order in which there is both abject poverty and gross wealth. In his own time, Jesus roundly attacked the injustices when the rich and powerful lauded it over the poor and powerless. Nothing has changed in our own world of today where we still see such injustice, for instance, where we see the present economic crisis has led to unemployment of so many and the paying off those whose greed was chiefly responsible for the economic collapse. The vision of society which we see in the life and teaching of Jesus is that all should share life to its full, not only in his own time but in all times including the world of today.

Violence and Peace

Today we live in a world of increasing violence and warfare. In the Middle East men, women and children are being killed daily as they battle in the name of religion, culture and oil. Countries in Africa are falling apart as warring groups battle for control. Parents of the dead mourn for their loved ones on both sides of such violence. Some years ago in Africa, I witnessed a small family gathered around the grave of the father who had been killed by terrorists the night before. My wife and I wept with them as the Bishop prayed. Many others had been killed and, on the way home, we were held up by a group of teenagers armed with rifles, all pointed at us. The bishop spoke to one of them whom he had confirmed only a few weeks before and we were then allowed to pass. This is not the will of God. We were told by Jesus to "love our enemies." These are not just comfortable words but a powerful command. On the positive side today, many of the world's leaders gather together to discuss the challenges that face us all and try to work for a more just and peaceful world but, at the same time, such leaders also continue to develop and use vast stocks of armaments including nuclear devices. Much of the violence is the result of abject poverty, cultural and religious extremism and the scramble for such resources as oil, gold and other valuable resources. The challenges are huge as we continue to pray and work for an end to violence and for justice and peace in God's world.

Race

There is absolutely no doubt that, in God's eyes, there is absolutely no distinction between people of different races on the earth. All are equal in the eyes of God. There is no single word in the Bible for *race* or *racism*. Sadly, this has not always been the view of the Church. The Church of the 18th and 19th in Europe was blind to the extent to which human slaves were being sent from their ancestral homes to America and in their attitude towards black people in their own society in Europe, especially in England. It was not until the practice was challenged by leaders like Wilberforce who insisted that black and white were equally love by God that the slave trade was faced and dealt with. It was echoed 200 years later by Martin Luther king, who was himself to pray the price of his own life for his actions. Even today, the dark shadow of racism remains and expresses itself in the so-called *immigrant crisis* in so many of today's societies. Certainly, there will always be differences of culture, religion, colour and language but they should not be allowed to influence the underlying reality that we are all *children of God* and that we all share our human reality. Maybe the acceptance of Obama to the Presidency of the United States will lead to a growing development of a society in which religion, colour or culture will cease to lead to dissension and violence in tomorrow's world.

The Challenge of a Rapidly Changing World

I must conclude with the huge challenge to do with the many issues related to climate change and the future of our planet earth. Some three thousand years ago, the African Sahara was a land of many people, sustained by the well-watered and productive landscape. Then, quite suddenly, the climate changed. The crops all died and the soil became the desert which we know today, leaving its people to move into the lush Nile Valley which came to be called Egypt. Today we are faced with similar challenges which embrace the whole world in which we all live. If the human race is to survive, we must face up to the challenges which will continue to face all our children and their descendents. Just as the people of the Sahara were face with the drying up of water, so now our human race is threatened with a multitude of challenges in today's world.

Climate change is already to be seen in the warming up of the North and South Poles, which is having widespread effects, not only in the possible loss of certain species but also the growing political attempts to own the newly open seas and sources of minerals. We are faced with the diminishing sources of oil, coal and other resources and the inevitable claims on the ownership. We are witnessing the slow destruction of trees and other growing species which are such an importance in today's world. We are facing the affects of chemical materials on productive land and the rapid growth of building in a world in which the population growth is rapidly expanding. We are also challenged with the effects of violence in today's society and the growing strength and power of today's weapons of mass destruction.

Just how can we, as Christians, help our world to deal with these challenges and give it hope for the growing 21st century? How can we use all the amazing discoveries of science for the betterment of us all in the future? There are certainly no simple answers but I would like to suggest some ideas so that all the discoveries of the modern world can become ways of leading us into a more just and compassionate community. Clearly we need to develop further sources of energy to take the place of the inevitable shrinking of those we have at present. We need to develop the God given powers of water, wind, sun and possibly nuclear power. The future will probably mean the increasing involvement of governments in developing such things as the use of land, the growth of buildings and the planning of transportation. We will need to change and adapt some of our traditional ways that we eat and how we travel. In all of this, we must also work towards a world of justice and peace in which all will be able share in the world that God has given us. As we look forward, we live in hope and pray that we and our descendents will overcome all of these challenges as we open our minds and hearts to the vision of a world as God would have it. The vision of the Kingdom of God, here in our own world, is indeed at the heart of the Christian faith. As Kenneth Leech, the much respected English theologian was to put it: "The Kingdom of God means not only a personal but also a social and cosmic transformation. God not only wants to transform each one of us but the cosmos we inhabit."

I would like to end by stressing the critical importance of what I have written in the last two chapters of this book, the first focusing on our own personal transformation and the second pointing a vision of the vast world in which we all live. In fact, they are not separate but co-joined, just as our minds and bodies work together as one. If we open our minds and heart to the reality and presence of the Something More in our own lives, then we shall not only come to sense and recognize the beauty and wonder of our world but also our ability to either enhance or destroy it. As we draw individually closer to God, we shall endeavour to do all we can to enhance the natural world around us, we shall see science not as a way of destroying and stripping the planet's resources but see that they are treated with care and respect, we shall look upon our fellow human beings as brothers and sisters, both in our own communities and throughout the world. Finally, we must assume our place in sharing and becoming involved in bringing these things to be. Our faith is not just for our personal benefit. We are all members of one world and we are all responsible for its future. To know God is to be not only open ourselves to God in our own lives but to be co-sharers in building the Kingdom of God in whatever ways we can.

Further Reading

Borg, Marcus J., and N. T. Wright. *The Meaning of Jesus: Two Visions.* San Francisco: Harper, 1999.

Cullman, Oscar. *The State in the New Testament.* London: S.C.M., 1957.

Gore, Al. *Earth in the Balance: Ecology and the Human Spirit.* Emmaus, PA: Roledale Press, 2006.

Ingham, Michael. *Mansions of the Spirit: The Gospel in a Multifaith World.* Toronto: Anglican Book Centre, 1997.

Jenkins, Philip. *The Next Christendom: The Rise of Global Christianity.* Oxford: Oxford University Press, 2002.

Leech, Kenneth. *Subversive Orthodoxy: Traditional Faith and Radical Commitment.* Toronto: Anglican Book Centre, 1992.

Leech, Kenneth. *The Sky is Red.* London: Darton, Longman and Todd Ltd., 1997.

Mayendorf, John. *Bysantine Theology: Historical Trends and Doctrinal Themes.* New York: Fordham University Press, 1978.

Polkinghorne, John. *The Way the World is: The Christian Perspective of a Scientist.* Louisville: Westminster John Knox Press, 2007.

Richardson, Alan. *The Political Christ.* London: S.C.M., 1976.

Schnell, Jonathan. *The Fate of the Earth.* New York: Knopf, 1982.

Temple, William. *Christianity and Social Order.* New York: Seabury Press, 1976.

Theissen, Gerd. *Sociology of Early Palestinian Christianity.* Philadelphia: Fortress Press, 1978.

Theissen, Gerd. *The Shadow of the Galilean.* Philadelphia: Fortress Press, 1978.

Vermes, Geza. *The Religion of Jesus the Jew.* Minneapolis: Fortress Press, 1993.

Chapter 8
Something More

I have added here three personal experiences which have had a profound significance in my life which, I believe, give special weight to my belief there is in fact *something more* than the purely physical world in which we all live. The first two I personally experienced in my own life. The third is an amazing experience of my son, an experience which was radically to change his life.

"You Have Saved My Life"

One day, right after the Sunday Eucharist in my Winnipeg church, I saw a couple of young black men coming up the aisle to meet me. One of them grasped me by the hand and said: "I want to thank you for saving my life." Now this was not your usual "I enjoyed your sermon" kind of remark and I was totally taken back. I had no idea what he was talking about but, over the next few days I was to find out. This was his story as confirmed later by his family while my wife and I were in Uganda.

George, as he was called, had been a student at Makarere University in the capital city of Kampala. He had been studying English and was an active student on the campus. One evening, a company of Ugandan soldiers had broken into his residence, seized George, thrown him into the back of an army truck and driven him away. Uganda at that time was under the brutal rule of Premier Milton Obote and in a state of civil war. His prime weapon was the army which exercised a brutal wave of terror on all who opposed him. Because George had been somewhat outspoken in criticism, he had been singled out for punishment and this lead to his arrest at the University. The truck had been driven some miles out of Kampala to a clearing at a place where there was a memorial to some martyrs who had been massacred during the past century. There it stopped and George was dragged from the truck. He was bound and led away to the edge of the clearing, where the soldiers formed a firing squad in front of him. Before they went any further, George asked them to allow him to say a few words. They then waited as he related how he forgave them for what they were about to do. When he was finished, they raised their rifles and shot him. Then, as he was still moving, one of them threw a grenade at him and left him for dead. He told me they heard something coming and fled in their truck. George was badly wounded but not dead and, as soon as the soldiers had gone, a young boy who had been hiding in the bushes went to get help. He went on to tell me how his rescuers managed to get him to a hospital, where his wounds were treated. In the meantime, the army had heard of his escape and came looking for him in the hospital but they were too late. His Christian friends had managed to smuggle him out and, in the days which followed, had managed to get him out of the country to a refugee camp in nearby Kenya. There, his wounds were patched up and he was safe but his future was slim, especially in light of his badly wounded state. It was highly unlikely that any country would give him asylum and there was little hope of ever getting away from the camp. Then one day he received a summons to the camp office and was told that an agreement had been reached with the Canadian Visa Officer for George to be admitted to Canada under the Canadian Refugee Programme of the time. What was highly unusual was that Canada's criteria for such admissions virtually eliminated any applicants with such severe injuries as George's. However, he relayed that a letter had been received from a priest in Canada called Ian Stuchbery, whose parish had offered to take responsibility for such an applicant who would not otherwise qualify for admission. He was received from the camp, put on a plane for Canada and duly arrived in Ottawa.

By the time he got there, details of the letter had got lost and the question of where George was to go was debated. Quite by chance, George found himself on a plane to Winnipeg, where he was met by a worried immigration officer who had been given no instructions as to how to deal with this badly injured individual, so that he was put, together with a pair of Ugandans, in a compartment and left to himself. However, George was an Anglican and, shortly after their arrival, the three of them found out where the nearest Anglican church was and came along the next Sunday. On their first visit, they simply slipped quietly away together with a copy of the weekly bulletin. When they got back to their apartment, George happened to read the name of the Rector, "the Rev Ian Stuchbery." He remembered the name from the remark of the officer at the refugee camp and so there he was the following Sunday, rushing up the aisle to greet me with the words, "You have saved my life!"

The story did not end there. George was still severely wounded. His wounds required extensive surgery, especially the repairing of the many nerves which had been wounded. And there was no question (possibility?) of his obtaining work in a strange country. The parish was in a difficult situation since, although George had been accepted by Canadian Immigration, there was no money provided by them to pay for the massive surgery which was necessary. In the meantime, here was George and we felt somewhat helpless. Then things began to break. One of the people in the parish was a senior surgeon at the large general hospital, who also happened to be Chairman of the national Primate's World Relief and Development Fund, which was responsible for refugee work in the Anglican Church. As a result, George was able to get first class treatment in the major hospital in the city, which left him almost fully recovered except for a slight handicap in one arm. But George still needed a job and to look after himself in a strange country. This led to the second *co-incidence*. The subject which George had been studying at University in Uganda was English and, while in university, he had acquired something for himself as an actor. But how could the parish help? Quite by chance, a member of our refugee committee was Nancy, an actress very much involved with the Prairie Theatre exchange, a vibrant and successful theatre in Winnipeg at the time. She managed to get George a job and, from them on, it was all that George needed.

Time went on and my wife and I were living in Montreal and we had lost all touch with George. Then, one night, we happened to see him in a TV movie and we discovered that he had gone from success to success. Not long afterwards, we went to a local theatre where George was performing in a play written by him, telling his story. It was a moving experience and we had the pleasure of seeing him after the show and we asked each other, was all this simply *synchronicity* or the response of a loving God to a letter sent in faith?

"She is My Mother!"

Some time later, the parish had written to the Visa Officer at the Embassy offering to assist another refugee who had some kind of disability which would otherwise prevent her admission to Canada. Some weeks later, I received a letter asking us whether we would be willing to receive a mother and her fourteen year old daughter. They had arrived at the Nairobi camp from Ethiopia, which was then at war with Somalia.

Laura, the mother was an Ethiopian Christian who had been living in an area which had been subject to frequent bombing by the Somali Air Force. One day, their home received a direct hit from a napalm bomb. As a result all her family except for herself and her twelve year old daughter was killed. She escaped injury but her daughter received terrible wounds to most of her body, which left her severely disfigured. But, shortly afterwards, both mother and daughter were captured by some Somali forces in a cross border raid and taken to a camp. There, as Christians, they had been reviled as unclean and the daughter had been treated with contempt because of her disfigurement. However, they had escaped to Kenya where they were now in a refugee camp. There was no way they would be accepted by Canadian Immigration unless a group would be prepared to be responsible for them here. The officer asked whether we would be willing to give that guarantee. I gave her the assurance that we would.

So far, so good but there was *something more* to come. Some months later, before the two arrived in Canada, I was idly perched on a table in the Winnipeg Immigration Office and recounting the story to the woman at the desk and hardly noticed a young man who was sitting right across from me. As I got into conversation with him and told him my story, I noticed the colour drain from his face and, when I had finished he hesitatingly asked me the mother's name. I told him "Laura." There was a huge pause and them he said to me, very quietly, "She is my mother."

In fact, it turned out that she was not in fact his natural mother but the one who had adopted him when his original mother had been killed. She had taken him into her own family and, when the soldiers had later taken her away, he had given her up for dead. It was a moment which hung in the air and I shall never forget it. When Laura and her daughter arrived in Winnipeg, it was her adopted son who greeted her at the airport. Another *God instance*? I believe so.

John's Story

One of the most powerful stories in the New Testament is that which is usually described as the Conversion of St Paul. It tells how he was on a journey towards Damascus in order to put a stop to the new *Jesus* movement which was threatening the authorities at the time. He was recorded as having a vision on the way to the city of Damascus, an experience which was to change his life and the course of history.

My final story was almost as dramatic and it was experienced by one of my sons. With his permission, I have decided to include it as a post-script, since it so powerfully illustrates an experience of the Something More, an experience which was to heal him and radically to change his whole life. The story tells of how, right from his early years, he had found the concept of God as being "pretty ridiculous." From then onwards he described himself as an atheist, or as he himself describes it: "I flirted with agnosticism from time to time, keeping up the appearance of a 'clergy kid' and being a very active church member."

After his school years, he left home and tells of how he "abandoned the last vestige of my socially acceptable upbringing." In the seven years that followed, his life went downhill. He recounts how he "went through vast quantities of marijuana and hash and became addicted to cocaine." And then, something quite amazing was to happen, which was to change his whole life radically. He had reached a point which he himself describes as an "ongoing experience of despair, broken only by the brief high of cocaine or the sleepy haze of marijuana or hash." Then, one afternoon, he experienced something which was to change his whole life. As he now describes it, he recalls how "the intensity of my despair was particularly horrendous as my addiction ran my life and controlled my body." Though he had long before denied the existence of God, at this point in his desperation he now turned to God and spoke what he called "his first real prayer: 'God, if you are real, then help me; please get me out of this place!'"

Chapter 8

What happened at that point was as dramatic as the experience of Paul on the road to Damascus. John describes it as a frightening vision of "two cold, empty black eyes" staring at him and a voice saying, "You are mine!" Then John tells of another voice from behind him and feeling a warm presence. Then he heard this second voice calling him, saying how it loved him, and saw a hand being extended towards him. He describes how a strange feeling of peace came over him and he continues: "The incident marked the end of my addiction to cocaine." He goes on to recount how over the next two years, he slowly came to know God in the person of Jesus Christ.

John recounted this amazing story to us some time after, during which time he had undergone a radical change. My wife and I noticed the change which expressed itself in the output of music he composed, in which he told of God's power to heal and transform. Some time later, he spoke to my wife and me about his sense that God was calling him to be a priest, a call that was fulfilled some years later. His whole life had been changed by the *Something More*. God was indeed real. I will end with some brief words that he later wrote: "My growing continues and ends with God. I know that, until then, I try to listen to that guiding voice of Jesus, a voice I know I can trust."

Some Biblical Words

One of the results of Biblical studies has been to clarify many of the words which have played a significant role in helping us better to understand the message of Jesus. Some of the often used words have become *buzz words* in our society which are used to describe what we believe about God and how to live our daily lives. Sadly, many of these buzz-words have often been used inappropriately in argument and discussion over the course of time and through translation. As a result, many of them need to be re-examined anew so as to reveal their true meanings. Here are some of the important words about which we need to be clear.

SIN: Perhaps the most difficult word to apply in our own day. In the original Hebrew context, it was a word used to describe any act that was seen to be against the will of God and God's laws. It was therefore seen in the context of the Law courts and so seen as leading inevitably to retribution and punishment. This certainly made sense if we only had an image of God as the angry judge, pointing his finger in judgment. However, if we are to accept the image of God as revealed in Jesus and as the "father with the open arms" (see chapter 6), then we are given a deeper insight into the word *sin*. Sin can be understood as the basic egocentricity within each one of us as human beings and thus the basic source of human greed and violence. What we see in the God of Jesus is not the fiery judge but the loving father (see chapter 6) who wants each of us to be *whole*, to be saved from our own self-centeredness and to be opened to receive the fullness of His infinite love.

SALVATION: (Latin salvatio) a word meaning *salving* or *making whole*. It is related to the word *healing* and it is in this sense that it is used in the New Testament.

LOVE: In the Greek language, which is the language in which the New Testament was written, there are three distinct words to express the English word love. The first is eros which is used only to describe sexual attraction. The second is the Greek word *philia* which corresponds to the English phrase *brotherly/sisterly* love or, more simply, *friendship*. The third is the Greek word *agape,* meaning altruistic love. It is the only word in the New Testament used to describe the character of God. It was used by some observers of the early church when they observed just how much the Christians "loved one another."

COMPASSION: Literally, it meant to *suffer with,* very similar to the word *agape* above. It was also used to describe the self-giving love of Jesus as he gave his life on the cross.

FORGIVENESS: Basically meaning to loose, let go, cancel or pardon. It is most powerfully exemplified in the parable of the forgiving father who welcomes his wayward son home.

MERCY: From the Hebrew word *tsedeth* which means kind or benevolent expressed in the same parable as above. It reflects the fundamental character of God, a God whose will is to be essentially compassionate and merciful despite all the sins of our human lives.

The Author

Ian Stuchbery is a retired Archdeacon in the Anglican Church of Canada. He was born in England and studied at Cambridge University before his further studies at McGill University and the Diocesan College in Montreal. Following his ordination, he served in two parishes in England before returning to Montreal as Vicar of the Cathedral. From there he continued his ministry as a parish priest in the major cities of Montreal, Winnipeg and Vancouver. Over the period of his ministry he experienced the exciting times of renewal within the Church but he also became aware of all the challenges facing the Church in today's increasingly secular world. He was also involved in the wider ministry of the Canadian Church and served for many years on various national committees concerning overseas development, worship, ministry and education in the Church. Serving on these committees provided opportunities to experience the ministry of the Anglican Church both in Canada and in other parts of the world. He has written two other books the last of which has been widely read and used throughout the Canadian Church and is in the process of its second revision.

Ian and his wife Sylvia have three children and ten grandchildren. One of their sons is a parish priest in Western Canada. They now live in retirement with their beloved dog in Nova Scotia and Prince Edward Island where they enjoy a busy life, both in a university town and in the delights of country and seaside.